EVOLUTION
Another False Religion of Humanism

By

Dennis D. Helton

ISBN: 978-1-7365344-2-7

All Scripture quotes are from the King James Bible

Address All Inquiries To:
THE OLD PATHS PUBLICATIONS, Inc.
142 Gold Flume Way
Cleveland, Georgia, U.S.A.

Web: www.theoldpathspublications.com
E-mail: TOP@theoldpathspublications.com

DEDICATION

To my six daughters, Debbie, Donna, Dale, Denise, Deree, and Dena.

Dennis Helton
February 2021

TABLE OF CONTENTS

EVOLUTION
Another False Religion of Humanism

Contemporary philosophy and vain deceit

Since leading *humanists* have publicly admitted that **evolution is a religion** (*The Voice in the Wilderness,* p. 10, June-July 2003), there is a need to counteract this religion's false tenets lest the naïve and those "dull of hearing" of truth be further deluded. Properly defined, humanism and evolution are no more than updated versions of paganism. The Bible refutes the false **philosophies and traditions** of men as well as the worship of nature.

> *Colossians 2:8: Beware lest any man spoil you through **philosophy** and **vain deceit**, after the **tradition of men**, after the rudiments of the world, and not after Christ.*

Simply stated, evolution of "beginnings" (earth; heavens; vegetation; minerals; animals; man) is a vain philosophy of an unbeliever's world-view concerning the existence of earth and all that is in it.

Why evolution is not credible

1.) There is absolutely no tangible proof of any kind to support the evolution hypothesis.

It is accurate to say that evolution is no more than a philosophical world-view. It is mere "humanism" or more accurately, "atheism."

2.) The First Law of Thermodynamics (true science) refutes evolution: This law says, "Matter cannot be created nor destroyed but only changed in form."

The evolutionists always demand some form of **matter** to initiate their theory of beginnings such as: amino acids; green murky gases; stellar dust; primordial soup; unicellular animal; multi-cellular animal; monkey hanging from a tree; professor with a Ph.D. The evolutionists never even delve into where and how their gases, dust, amino acids, matter, etc. originated! Only God can *create* matter.

3.) The Second Law of Thermodynamics (true science) refutes evolution: "The Law of Entropy S" says that all systems (open or closed) increase in entropy S (toward disorder) when no external forces act upon them. The system tends to break down into the simplest elements; it does not build up into a more complex system.

This official law of true science is exactly opposite the false science of evolution. In nature, there is the strong propensity to break down, not build up.

4.) There are billions of fossils and none show a bridge between kinds. The gaps between kinds cannot be bridged. The kinds have many varieties within each kind.

If evolution had legs to stand on, there would have to be exceedingly far more transitional forms than basic kinds. Varieties or changes are not evolution origins.

5.) Many famed evolutionists admit that there is no fossil proof of evolution. There are no transitional forms.

In other words, evolutionists themselves have learned that there is no real scientific evidence for factual evolution of "origins." There is no evidence of "particles to people," "molecules to man," or "monkeys to men."

There are random reports of the discovery of fossils of men and apes that are said to be 150,000-1,000,000 years old. Strangely (not really) they have changed very little, if any at all, after those *alleged* millions of years. They closely resemble present day skeletal and fossil remains or else they could not even be identified and classified.

6.) There are no scientific proofs that evolution ever happened in the past nor are there observations of evolution occurring today; nether will evolution occur in the future.

Of course, proponents of creation did not observed the origin of life but neither did evolutionists! You either believe God's record of Creation or you believe the endless speculations of unreliable evolutionists. Evolution only occurs in the demented minds of fuzzy-brained professors and their naive protégés (students).

This writer never imagined that in his lifetime people would have the audacity to rise up and unashamedly publicly proclaim their descent from a monkey! Anyone believing this incredulous claim is definitely lacking in common sense; far more importantly, they are also openly refuting the Biblical record of Creation. They should be ashamed!

It is very evident that education does not remove the cobwebs of willing ignorance.

7.) There are billions of non-transitional structures; so where are the trillions of transitional forms needed to bridge the gaps?

The evolutionists are compelled to concede that no kind of animal suddenly changed into another kind. Again, the transitional forms demanded for changing from one kind to another would far exceed the basic kinds.

8.) The alleged men/chimps hybrids are *concocted* **from an assortment of jawbones, teeth, and fossilized scraps together with molecular evidence from living species. The scraps are pieced together to form a line of human descent** *allegedly* **going back 5-8 million years when humans and chimps diverged from a common ancestor.**

Fragments from fragments of diverse bone-scraps prove nothing.

9.) All evolutionary changes are horizontal or downward, never vertical or upward. They are toward deterioration and extinction, not toward complexity and improvement.

Variables and changes are not evolutions of beginnings; variables are changes within kinds.

(Evolution: The etymological definition of evolution was simply "an unrolling, or opening" from the Latin noun e*volutio*. This unrolling was in

10

reference to "changes" **within kinds**, not "origins or beginnings" of kinds.

Evolutionists, holding a greater sway and in control of modern public education, have changed the true meaning of "evolution of change" to "evolution of beginnings" to fit their private agenda.)

Genesis 1:24: *And God said, Let the earth bring forth the living creature* **after his kind**; *cattle, and creeping thing, and beast of the earth* **after his kind**: *and it was so.*

10.) Most evolutionists, having lost most of their debates with creationists, decline opportunities for scientific debates, and those that do debate prefer to make unilateral attacks on the creationists.

Since the facts do not support their position, evolutionists resort to throwing insults and slurs upon the intelligence and integrity of the creationists. Actually, this ploy is a smokescreen to cover up their "own" ignorance and ineptitude. Perhaps the application of "grandstanding" fits their tactics quite well!

(Yes, the writer knows that the insertion of "own" is not essential but desired an emphasis upon ignorance and ineptitude.)

11.) Evolutionists must believe in evolution; it is their religion. They believe it in spite of the lack of evidence, not because of it. Evolution of beginnings is *not science*, it is *a philosophical world-view*.

It is the evolutionist's religion; it is more than an ape-man, it is his own "created" straw-man (pun intended). Evolution when applied to mean "origins " is no more than *junk* science

12.) Evolutionists, themselves, have shown that evolutionism is not science but religious faith in atheism. They believe in evolution *because they want to*!

Don't confuse the evolutionists with glaring facts that refute their "monkey" business: for most of them, their minds are already made up.

When a certain evolutionist denied the Creation account of Adam and Eve, a preacher told him, "You have stumbled over a rib and swallowed a monkey."

13.) Evolutionists are not rational; they do not use common sense nor the light of the law of nature.

The heavens declare the glory of God (Psalms 19:1).

14.) Darwinian teachers and liberal left-wing professors must believe in evolution: their livelihoods (salaries) depend upon it.

They should get an honest job teaching truth.

15.) Atheists, evolutionists, and haters of God must have a crutch to lean upon or a security pillar for their *ailing faith*, so they choose evolution as their religion. Properly translated, this means that they believe that man is his own god (called "humanism").

The writer uses *ailing faith* to describe the unbeliever's religion because these evolutionists do have faith...of a sort. It takes **greater faith** to believe in the ridiculous, ludicrous, hypothesis of evolution, than to believe in Creation by Almighty God. Think about it!

The writer readily confesses that he does not have enough faith to believe in evolution of "beginnings." Evolution is a dead end. All people have faith in something; however, the faith of the prideful atheists and evolutionists is resting upon sinking sand rather than the Rock of salvation, Jesus Christ.

16.) The fossil record assures us that life did not begin by evolution. Fossils show that life appeared on earth suddenly and fully formed.

The possibility of life beginning naturalistically (evolutionary) and forming mature complex life-systems from inanimate matter is too absurd to consider. Our miracle-working Creator God is the answer. Proud man thinks he has the answer.

The surest discredit for evolution

The surest and most important reason for discounting evolution is simply because the Word of God declares that **God created the world** and everything in it in six literal solar 24-hour days (Genesis 1:3-27; Exodus 20:11; 31:17).

Psalms 33:6, 9: *By the word of the LORD were the heavens made; and all the host of them by the*

13

breath of his mouth. For he spake, and it was done; He commanded, and it stood fast.

What about 'so-called' theistic evolution?

Theistic evolution is sometimes referred to as "progressive evolution." Creation and evolution have opposite meanings. Theistic Evolution is an *oxymoron* (word contradiction term) such as, "Deafening silence," Winning loser," and "Honest crook."

Creation: embodies an instantaneous operation of a very brief time; the creation of minerals, mature animals (with seed after his kind), and mature vegetation (with seed after his kind) from waters and earth (Genesis 1:20-25). Of course, God created the waters and earth. The only true and wise God of the Bible also created man (male and female) of the dust of the ground (Genesis 2:7; 5:2) in His own image, in the image of God (Genesis 1:27). Creation was of supernatural origin, not of natural processes.

Evolution: embodies millions and billions of years; trillions and trillions of basic stellar substance to supply a hypothetical beginning, an incredible faith in nothing, a zillion tons of luck, and an empty head to believe that inanimate matter was the brains behind it all.

Evolutionists at first claimed that evolution of origins began **millions of years ago**. The present claim by some evolutionists has now escalated to **billions of years ago**. As facts continue to erode their evolution fantasy, the writer supposes we can eventually expect the evolutionist to claim **trillions of years ago**.

If "so-called" theistic evolution of man (millions of years) is a plausible hypothesis, then someone tell this writer why the Almighty, Omniscient, Omnipotent Creator would wait such a long time to communicate with man who is the crown of His creation? Of course, the writer can answer that question for the theistic evolutionists. They would likely reply that man was then in the embryonic or monkey stage of development! The mentality of evolutionists is very predictable.

The writer is a "young earth" advocate of **thousands of years** (*about* 6,000 years).

Henry M. Morris says, "It is worth noting that, whenever the verbs *create* or *make* are used in reference to God's work of creation, they are never in the present tense. God is not now creating or making stars, or animals or people as *theistic evolution* requires; at the end of the six-day creation period, in fact, God 'rested' from all His work which God created and made" (Genesis 2:3).

Many evangelical Protestant Christians believe that they must conform to the un-scientific, un-provable hypothesis of evolution (or theistic evolution). **It is a sad fact that "so-called" theologians and anemic Bible scholars rely on secular scientists to interpret Scripture for them!** Opinions of unregenerate scientists are of more consequence to some "so-called" Christians than those of qualified creationist scientists.

The religious head of the Roman Catholic Church of a billion people (Pope John II) stated his belief in evolution shortly before he died.

According to the *Fundamentalist Digest,* January 2011, p. 18 (West Branch, MI 48661, December 2010) the present pope, Benedictine XVI (Joseph Ratzinger) in his book, *Truth and Tolerance,* approved theistic evolution. The writer does not believe that all Catholic people agree with the evolution of "beginnings."

Advocates of theistic evolution use an "alleged" gap theory that states that there was a pre-Adamite race of people upon earth between Genesis 1:1 and Genesis 1:2. The phony story goes something like this:

Demons—Spirits of a pre-Adamic race?

According to this field of thought, a pre-Adamic race existed on the original Earth before it became "dark and void" (Genesis 1:2). These humanlike creatures lived under the government of God and were presided over by Lucifer, the "anointed cherub that covereth" (Ezekiel 28:14). When these pre-Adamites joined Lucifer in revolt against God, a cataclysm fell upon Earth, physically destroying its inhabitants. Only the spirits of these beings survived to roam the earth disembodied. This is offered as an explanation for why demons desire to possess humans, as they were meant to be "housed" in bodies of flesh and are uncomfortable otherwise.

There could not have been a pre-Adamic race living on earth during the 6-day Creation Week because: 1.) "...God saw that it was good." -

Genesis 1:25; 2.) Since the first five days were pronounced by God as "good," no cataclysmic corruption led by Satan could have occurred during this time. 3.) If no cataclysm occurred during God's Creation spelled out in 6 24-hour days, two Creations would be demanded (one corrupted and one uncorrupted) and there is not a hint of two Creations in the Scriptures.

Of course, there was no earth yet formed in the middle of Day-One of Creation; hence no corruption could have occurred.

Again, neither is there any such thing as 'theistic evolution.' The term *theistic evolution* was coined by *religious* men who were either weak in the faith, ignorant of biblical teaching, or plainly unsaved (or perhaps those desiring to be politically correct). Those weak in the faith are often intimidated into compromising biblical creation by evolution scientists who sound dogmatic and authoritative. God did not use millions or billions of years to make the earth and all therein. The heavens and all the host of them were made by the Word of the LORD. He spake and it was done (Psalms 33:6- 9) in six literal 24-hour days. In the Genesis account of creation, we have the formula "first day, second day...morning and evening" repeated which define a 24-hour day (Genesis 1:5, 8, 13, 19, 23, 31). There are no "mornings and evenings" in days equaling thousands or millions of years. The Jews understood this quite well. They understood that the Sabbath day, the 7th day of the creation week, was a 24-hour period of rest, not one day a thousand-years long nor one day a million-years long. In Exodus (as well as other

17

passages), it is expressly stated, "...in six days (just like our 24-hour day), the LORD made heaven and earth...with the finger of God" (Exodus 31:17-18).

(Note: In the Bible, the Hebrew word *yom* and Greek word *hemera,* meaning one-day of 24 hours, can also symbolize *an indefinite* or *long period* of time. In the NT, we have an example in Second Peter:

> II Peter 3:8: But, beloved, be not ignorant of this one thing, that one day is with the Lord as a thousand years, and a thousand years as one day.

This is time from God's perspective: He owns all time. Of course, **if** the word "day" did not have a precise meaning of 24 hours, a figurative use of the word would be needless and meaningless.

According to Hebrew prophecy in the book of Daniel, we are given an example where **one day equals one year** (or, one week equals 7 years; 70 weeks equals 490 years).

> Daniel 9:24: "Seventy weeks (490 years) are determined upon thy people (Jews) and upon thy holy City (Jerusalem)..."

There are many other times in Scriptures that a day refers to a longer period of time than a 24-hour/day, but you will **not** see the term "morning and evening" as in the creation account in chapter 1 of Genesis. The writer believes that each one of the 7 days of the creation week was a 24/hour day and was given as a pattern for man to follow.

Mature organisms required for reproduction of the species

God created man (Adam) in His own image (Genesis 1:27) with the "character of age," **not** an amino acid, seed, embryo, or an ape.

All humans descended from the first man and woman (Adam and Eve), not from an ape-like creature as touted by theistic evolutionists.

Adam did not have the appearance of a new-born baby at the time of his creation. At the tender age of one-day old, Adam had the literal character, physical body, and appearance of a full-grown man. Adam was not born nor evolved; he was created mature. Of course, this flies in the face of "theistic evolution."

Reproduction itself demonstrates the necessity of the **whole** organism. When God created fruit trees, they were already bearing fruit. In each case, what God created was complete and fully functional right at the very beginning. Creation without the literal appearance and character of "age" is impossible for creation itself speaks of the whole completed entity. The minimum number of parts necessary for an organism to reproduce is the organism itself. The whole mature organism is vital. This is scientific fact that cannot be broken down to any smaller level.

How could organisms "arise" by increments until they can reproduce? **Dr. Randy J. Guliuzza**, P.E., M.D. says, "This fact is so indicting that evolutionists will push back with all kinds of arguments, but they will all cheat in their explanations. Every example

19

given will always start and end by using some vital things from the organism itself, so be looking for this. For example, yes, there is "in vitro fertilization," but that starts with donor egg and sperm and the embryo is returned to the normal realm of development" (*Acts and Facts*, September 2010, pp. 10,11).

Evolutionists (unbelievers) disregard the Word of God...to their own hurt (Revelation 20:11-15; 21:8).

World-views of religionists

▪ **Theists:** believe in the existence of One True God as the Creator of man and the world.

• **Monotheists**: believe correctly in one God but *may not* know Him as their Savior. Job's three friends *may have* fit this category (only God knows). The writer himself always believed in only one true God (of the Bible) even before he was born again and had defended that belief during secular discussions.

• **Humanists:** believe that they **are their own god** and depend upon their own merit. Humanism is a philosophy that usually rejects super-naturalism and stresses an individual's dignity and worth and capacity for self-realization through reason. Man is incurably religious. If he does not have a god of his own choosing to bow down to, he makes himself to be his own god. Humanism is the religion of Christ-rejecting Bible-denying haters of God.

• **Pantheists:** tolerate the **worship of all gods** (as at in the Roman and Grecian Empires). They equate God with the forces and laws of nature and the universe.

• **Polytheists:** believe in or worship more than one god (or many gods).

• **Atheists:** deny that there is a God. In Scriptures, the atheist is called a fool (Psalms 14:1). Atheists themselves are the biggest fools of nature for they deny the very God who gave them their existence. In principal, atheists are their own god.

• **Deists:** advocate a natural religion, emphasizing morality, and in the 18th century denying the interference of the Creator with the laws of the universe. They believe in a supreme being of some nature but do not acknowledge the Great Jehovah God of the Scriptures.

There are reports that Thomas Jefferson, our third president, was a deist of sorts, but he was not an atheist nor was he an evolutionist.

Of course, the conclusions of great men count for nought unless their opinions are predicated upon the Word of God.

• **Evolutionists:** blindly believe that they originally evolved "from molecules to man" by sheer luck and with the assistance of oodles of time (millions to billions of years). This "monkey to man" creature insists that he is without prejudice and highly intelligent.

• **Theistic-Evolutionists:** foolishly believe that God used millions (or billions) of years and the process of evolution to form the world, initiate life, and all things therein. These people are usually very weak in Scriptures and their faith is highly suspect. The writer has never met a dedicated Spirit-filled believer that advocated such an anti-biblical philosophy.

Recent creation is the Biblical world-view

D. Russell Humphreys, Ph.D., said, "According to evolutionists, Stone Age Homo Sapiens existed for 190,000 years before beginning to make written records about 4,000 to 5,000 years ago. Prehistoric man built megalithic (*of huge stone*) monuments, made beautiful cave paintings, and kept records of lunar phases. Why would he wait two thousand centuries before using the same skills to record history?"

> *Exodus 20:11: "**In six days the LORD made heaven and earth, the sea, and all that in them is**, and rested the seventh day: wherefore the LORD blessed the [seventh] day, and hallowed it."*

> *Exodus 31:17: It is a sign between me and the children of Israel for ever: **for in six days the LORD made heaven and earth**, and on the seventh day he rested, and was refreshed.*

> *Mark 2:27: "The Sabbath was made for man."*

Of course, the weekly Sabbath was a 24-hour day.

Jesus (who was at the Creation, having Himself created all things (John 1:1-3) taught that mankind was made essentially at the same time of the cosmos.

> Mark 10:6: *"from the beginning God...made them male and female."*

The "Beginning" was a reference to Genesis 1:26.

In referring to Adam's son, Abel, Jesus spoke of "the blood of all the prophets, which was shed from the **foundation of the world**" (Luke 11:50, 51). Satan, using Cain to slay Abel, "was a murderer **from the beginning**" (John 8:44).

> Acts 3:21: *"...God hath spoken by the mouth of all His holy prophets **since the world began."** (See Hebrews 11:3-4; Jude 14.)*

The Old Testament prophets are put at the beginning of creation. There is not the slightest suggestion of millions and billions of years anywhere in the Bible except for the existence of the eternal God and the future eternal life for the **genuine** believer.

(**Genuine:** used because many profess salvation that do not possess it. The world is full of phony religion. In the Bible, religion is usually alluded to in a negative sense with the exception in James 1:27.)

> Matthew 7:13-14: *Enter ye in at the strait gate: **for wide is the gate, and broad is the way, that leadeth to destruction, and many there be which go in thereat:** Because strait*

is the gate, and narrow is the way, which leadeth unto life, and few there be that find it.

How can the universe be young if the stars are old? If a star is a million light-years away from earth, would it not take a million light-years for its light to reach us?

When God created the stars, He could have simultaneously (at the same time) created the light reaching earth. This is similar to the maturity and completion of day-old fruit trees already producing fruit.

(Adam could not have eaten of the fruit trees of the Garden of Eden unless the trees were mature and already producing fruit: he would have starved to death waiting for the trees and the garden in Eden to mature and produce fruit. Of course, Adam himself was also mature and fully functional at one-day old.)

A star created fully functional would eliminate the required time necessary for the starlight to reach earth. Creation itself is miraculous. Adam could have seen the stars as soon as they were created if he himself had been created on the fourth day of the creation week (the stars were created on day #4 and Adam was created on day #6).

The writer is well aware that some creation advocates do not accept the viewpoint of light reaching the earth at the time of the stars' creation, but the writer has no problem with it (star light other than our sun was minor light). The disclaimers say that God Himself was the light until the light of the stars reached earth and undoubtedly that is true for the first three days. Of course, a star without its light reaching its potential distance is an unfinished creation. To this writer, the creation of stars was not complete unless they were functional and the starlight was reaching earth at the same time that they were made. If light from the stars was not reaching their intended destinations at the time of their creation, then their creation was not complete. Starlight reaching the earth upon creation is analogous to Adam created as a grown mature man and the fruit trees in the Garden of Eden already producing fruit at one-day of age. Neither does the writer have any problem believing that God was the light during the first three-four days of the creation week nor of any other time (Genesis 1:3-13).

One science source estimates the distance to the nearest star generally to be about 100 light-years. Based upon this distance, a time of 100 years would be required for the star's light to reach earth in **natural manner**. Light could not reach earth during the six-day creation period at this distance of 587 trillion miles. Of course, evolutionists assume that light has always traveled at the same speed as today (186,000 miles/second). It would have been no problem for God to have greatly accelerated the speed of light at the time of the creation of the stars because creation itself is miraculous.

Another science source postulates a distance of 24 trillion miles from the nearest star to earth. This is a much closer distance than the previous estimate of 587 trillion miles. If this distance were to be true for **all** of the stars, the time required time for light to reach the earth in **natural manner** would fall within the 6-day creation week. At a distance of 24 trillion miles, light would reach earth before Adam was created on the sixth day. However, without God miraculously causing the light to shine upon earth immediately at creation, the light from **distant stars** could not reach earth during the 6-day creation week. All of the stars (near and far) were created on the same day #4. It must be remembered that many stars are at distances of quadrillions of miles from earth. The time required for their light to reach earth in **natural manner** would be many years after the creation week was ended. Again, this would imply that Creation was unfinished or incomplete. God finished His Creation in six days (Genesis 2:1, 2). Again, since **all** of the stars were created on the same day #4 and the distance of many stars would prevent their light from reaching earth in natural manner within the creation week, the writer is compelled to believe that God caused the light from **all** of the stars, near and far, to reach earth at the very time of their creation.

The writer does not believe in the popular touted "Gap Theory." There was no large time-gap between Genesis 1:1 and Genesis 1:2 nor between the other creation days (though there are some wonderful Christians that hold to the time gap). The writer believes that all of the seven days of Creation Week were of the same length of 24-hours. How does the writer know this? The successive terms of "mornings and evenings" in the creation record of Genesis specify days of 24-hour length.

God's power is not restricted so as to need thousands or millions of years to finalize creation, and when He rested from His creation, it was not because He was tired or exhausted. God ended (ceased from) His creation because it was **finished in six days**. "THUS the heavens and the earth were finished, and all the host of them" (Genesis 2:1). God is a God of order, not disorder as in the 'big bang' of evolution.

(Light speed: Assuming a constant speed of light at 186,000 miles/second, the distance that light travels in one-light year is 5.87 trillion miles. We obtain this distance by multiplying 186,000 miles/second x 60 seconds/minute x 60 minutes/hour x 24 hours/day x 365 days/year = 5.865,696,000,000 trillion miles/year. Light travels 16,070, 400,000 billion miles in one day.)

Light reaching earth would be a different situation with our sun {which is considered a star}. The sun is only 93 million miles from the earth and light from it could reach earth in little over eight minutes. Light traveling at 186,000 miles/second extrapolates to a distance of 11,160,000 million miles in one minute. Dividing the 93,000,000 miles (distance to the sun) by 11,160, 000 miles/minute {distance light travels in one minute} equals 8.333 minutes.

The writer agrees that God Himself was the light {singular} before He made the two greater lights {plural}, the **sun** and **moon**, and also the stars (Genesis 1:3-5, 14-19).

Evolutionists and some theistic evolutionists presuppose that light has always traveled at the same speed (186,000 miles/second), which may not be true for the beginning of creation. Again, creation itself is miraculous and God could have easily accelerated star-light speed or used some other method. Evolutionists only recognize "naturalism" and reject the supernatural workings of God in Creation. Even plants sprouted and matured at supernatural speed during the six-day creation week, so it would be of no great wonder if God accelerated the speed of starlight supernaturally!

One writer (perhaps a "theistic evolutionist") says, "Let's say that a star is 1 million light-years away. The light from that star has traveled at the speed of light to reach us. Therefore, it has taken the star's light 1 million years to get here, and the light we are seeing was **created** 1 million years ago. So the star we are seeing is really how the star looked **a million years ago**, not how it looks today. In the same way, our sun is eight light-minutes away. If the sun were to suddenly explode right now, we wouldn't know about it for eight minutes because that is how long it would take for the light of the explosion to get here."

All of the stars (near and far) were all created on day # 4 (as were the sun and the moon); thus, starlight reaching the earth instantly appears to be a more reasonable answer for a short 6-day/24-hour creation period. The writer does not accept the idea that God continued to create stars beyond the fourth day of the 6-day creation week.

Again, creation itself is miraculous and far beyond man's finite comprehension.

Pastor Charles H. Spurgeon, said,

"I believe in science, but not in what is called 'science.' No proven fact in nature is opposed to revelation. The petty speculations of the pretentious we cannot reconcile with the Bible, and would not if we could. I feel like the man who said, 'I can understand in some degree how these great men have found out the weight of the stars, and their distances from one another, and even how, by the spectroscope, they have discovered the materials of which they are composed: but, said he, "I cannot guess how they found out their names." Just so, the fanciful part of science, so dear to many, is what we do not accept. That is the important part of science to many—that part which is a mere guess, for which the guessers fight tooth and nail. The mythology of science is as false as the mythology of the heathen; but this is the thing which is made a god of. I say again, as far as its facts are concerned, science is never in conflict with the truths of holy Scripture, but the hurried deductions drawn from those facts, and the inventions classed as facts, are opposed to Scripture, and necessarily so, because falsehood agrees not with truth" (*Science Falsely So-Called*, pp. 19, 20, Published by: Institution for Authority Research, Box 233, Herndon, KS 67739).

Jesus confirmed a "recent" creation age

*Mark 10:6: But from **the beginning of the creation** God made them male and female.*

EVOLUTION: ANOTHER FALSE RELIGIION OF HUMANISM

Here again, Adam and Eve are placed at the beginning of creation. The beginning of Creation and Adam and Eve was not 4.6 billion years ago as most evolutionists speculate. It must be remembered that antiquity of age was inherent in Creation. God did not initiate life starting with seeds or some form of icons, but He created mature biological organisms "whose seed is in itself" (Genesis 1:11). It should not be overlooked: Creation itself ("beginnings") was not an act of naturalism, it was a miraculous act of God.

The Antediluvian World

By reckoning from the genealogies and births in Genesis 5:1-30; 8:6, 11, it can be determined that Noah's flood occurred *about* the year 1,656 after the creation of Adam. Indeed, this supports a young earth of less than 10,000 years (the writer believes *about* 6,000 years). Of course, the earth had the appearance of great age in the very beginning of creation; if only basic elements were present, there would be no age-design or no growth indication of Creation (mature plants, mature animals, and mature man).

(**Note:** the writer italicizes the word, *about,* to assure the reader that this writer is not claiming to be the final authority {and of course, like the evolutionist, was not present at the beginning}; however, the writer is convinced beyond any doubt that his figures are far more accurate than the millions and billions of years postulated by the evolutionists. Those who accept the evolutionary geological ages are actually 'flying in the face of God' by rejecting His Word, whether intentionally or in pagan ignorance.)

Adam the first man, who lived to be 930 years old, lived *about* eight generations (726 years) before the world-wide flood came upon the earth. God promised that He would not again **destroy the earth** with a flood which indicated that the flood of Noah's day was **global,** not regional or localized. Besides, there have been many regional and localized floods since Noah's flood, and a local or regional flood would not destroy the earth.

> *Luke 11:50-51: That the blood of all the prophets, which was shed from the foundation of the world, may be required of this generation; From the blood of Abel unto the blood of Zacharias, which perished between the altar and the temple: verily I say unto you, It shall be required of this generation.*

Here Abel, the second son of Adam, is called a prophet and was in the "beginning of the foundation of the world," which was not 4.6 billion years ago. You either believe the Bible account concerning Creation or you are trusting in the secular rants and ravings of unbelieving evolutionists. There is no middle ground.

> *Matthew 12:30: He that is not with me is against me; and he that gathereth not with me scattereth abroad.*

Anyone choosing to believe in the pagan philosophy of 'evolution of beginnings' thereby rejecting God's Word on the matter of Creation, is certainly "not with God." They may profess to be a "Christian evolutionist," but that is another oxymoron (word contradiction). The Bible nowhere supports "theistic evolution." If a person dares to believe the anemic words of an evolutionist above God's record of creation and salvation, he is calling God a liar. Woe to him!

> *I John 5:9-12: If we receive the witness of men, the witness of God is greater: for this is the witness of God which he hath testified of his Son. He that believeth on the Son of God hath the witness in himself:* <u>*he that believeth not God hath made him a liar;*</u> *because he believeth not* <u>*the record*</u> *that God gave of his Son. And* <u>*this is the record,*</u> *that God hath given to us eternal life and this life is in his Son. He that hath the Son hath life; and he that hath not the Son of God hath not life.*

The same Bible record that teaches salvation by trusting in God's Son is the same record declaring Creation and *"all Scripture is given by inspiration of God"* (2 Timothy 3:16).

If the millions and billions of years claimed by evolutionists were to be true, then a legitimate claim could be made that God has lied to us; but God clearly tells us in His Word that He made everything in six literal 24/hour days. We know that God is pure and holy and cannot lie (Titus 1:2; Hebrews 6:18). Again, evolutionists are willingly ignorant; when they **choose** to follow a lie.

Secular scientists falsely date fossils (hardened remains of plant or animal life) to be many millions of years old

Death did not occur *before* Adam who certainly was not millions of years old. Sin and death only occurred *after* Adam sinned (Romans 5:12). This discounts the claims of evolutionists. Again, this boils down to puny, arrogant men standing against God's Word and rejecting His love.

> *I Corinthians 15:21: For since by man came death, by man came also the resurrection of the dead. For as in Adam all die, even so in Christ shall all be made alive.*

> *Romans 5:12: Wherefore, as by one man sin entered into the world, and death by sin; and so death passed upon all men, for that all have sinned.*

This discounts the long, long ages required of evolution. Too, petrifying and fossilizing does not require millions of years. There are documented cases of petrified wood in a very short time.

Will the solar system burn out?

> *Daniel 12:3: And they that be wise shall shine as the brightness of the firmament; and they that turn many to righteousness as the stars for ever and ever.*

> *Psalms 148:3, 6: Praise ye him, sun and moon: praise him, all ye stars of light. He hath also stablished them for ever and ever: he hath made a decree which shall not pass.*

Because of sin, *"the whole creation groaneth ...until now"* (Romans 8:22), and the heavens *"shall wax old as doth a garment...and they shall be changed"* (Hebrews 1:11-12).

Don't worry about the solar system burning out! Of course, the earth and its heavens (not the sidereal heaven or stars) will one day "pass away" (Matthew 24:35) and then will be changed by God into "new heavens and a new earth" (2 Peter 3:13) that will never pass away.

The effect upon population if man is millions of years old

Populations can grow very rapidly. Assuming that each family had six children, the seventy who came into Egypt with Jacob (Genesis 46:27) could easily have multiplied to 3-5 million in just ten generations. Actually, the total population was probably between two and three million at the time of the exodus from Egypt. There were 603,550 male adults that were able to go to war (Numbers 1:46) not including the priestly tribe of Levi.

According to Charles Darwin's simple geometric growth rate ("struggle for existence" in nature), it would only take about 1,100 years to develop the present world population of six billion people (assuming 35 years per generation). It has been over 4,000 years since the global flood. With man's long life span still prevailing and with large agrarian families, the population would have grown explosively. One person has humorously stated that people would be clinging to the edge of earth ready to fall off due to over-population.

In answer to this population extrapolation, the scholar, **Dr. Henry M. Morris** says,

> "All of which indicates that the evolutionary scenario, which assumes that human

populations have been on the earth for about a million years, is absurd. The whole universe could not hold all the people" (*Days of Praise*, June-July, August 2002, p. 5).

Evolution hypothesis in former years

In the late forties and early fifties when this writer was in public high school (*Westville High School*, Greenville, SC), the science classes had little to say concerning evolution. The only mentioning of evolution was the "Nebular Hypothesis." The science teachers had such little regard for evolution that they apologized for having to even mention it and only did so because it was in the science textbook.

(**Nebular Hypothesis:** a theory advanced by the French astronomer Pierre Simon Laplace {1749-1827} to explain how our solar system was formed. He said the sun and planets were formed from a nebula, or cloud of intensely heated gas. Gravitation caused the nebula to condense and form globes -- *World Book Encyclopedia*, Volume 14, Copyright 1980, U.S.A.)

A late hypothesis of evolution (similar to the 'nebular hypothesis') is called the *Big Bang conjecture/guess* (the writer refuses to dignify this pagan philosophy with the word "theory"). In other words, the universe came into being due to a giant explosion. Even an imbecile (dimwit; nincompoop) can see the contradiction in an evolution that requires multiplied millions (or billions) of years followed by a gigantic evolutionary explosion that formed **incomprehensible complex life** and **innumerable galaxie systems** suddenly **in great order**! Whenever has an explosion created order? Explosions destroy and tear down! And where did the chemicals come from? Who designed the explosion? Who ignited the huge firecracker? Where did the heat come from? Where did the stars, suns, or gases come from? Any rational person would have a hard time swallowing this hodge-podge (mess)! Of course, the evolutionists irrationally want it any way that fits their ungodly humanistic philosophy. The great Creator God even created the poor evolutionist (without his unbelief...which was acquired). For sure, much did appear suddenly but it was by the Word of God's power (Hebrews 1:3).

Numerous conjectures of evolution cancel out all others. It is said that the science books of evolutionists have to be rewritten every ten years.

The evolution philosophies of beginnings are generally divided into three chronological ages:

1. -past evolution which has ceased (no evidence to support it)

2. -present evolution occurring now (no evidence to support it)

3. -future evolution which will resume at some future time (no evidence to support it)

Remember, evolutionists are talking about evolution of "beginnings," not evolution of "changes." No one contests evolution of changes; variations are evident in every generation. If an evolutionist chooses any one of numerous evolutionary hypotheses of the three ages (past; present; future), he automatically cancels out all other natural mechanisms making them null and void (of course, all are phony). Mr. Unbeliever, take your pick of the many speculations and varied claims of evolution.

Unbelievers are risking the loss of their **everlasting** soul upon the frail and forever vacillating philosophies of evolutionists that frequently change (every ten years). There are only two **everlasting** habitats for man, Heaven or Hell.

> *Matthew 25:41, 46: Then shall he say also unto them on the left hand, Depart from me, ye cursed, into **everlasting fire**, prepared for the devil and his angels: And these shall go away into **everlasting punishment**: but the righteous into life eternal.*

The above Scriptures of Matthew 25 makes the future very clear for all to see. If the unbeliever is correct in his faith in evolution and we all die (unbelievers and believers), then nothing is lost of either and we are all as dead dogs; however, if evolutionists are wrong and creationists are correct and we all die, the righteous will inherit **life eternal** in Heaven and the unrighteous will go away into **everlasting punishment in the lake of fire**. Why would a rational person risk losing his soul in order to comply with varied, unproven, and "far-out" philosophies of vain, fallible men? The inherent pride of man will cause many the loss of their soul.

Dr. Henry M. Morris said,

"The overwhelming commitment to evolutionism is not because of the scientific evidence, but rather because of antipathy (strong or deep-rooted dislike; aversion) to biblical Christianity. Even **Charles Darwin** became an evolutionist and agnostic because

37

of his rejection of the biblical doctrine of **divine punishment"** (Acts and Facts, Nov. 2010, *Biology and the Bible*, p. 4)

Again, both evolution and creation are matters of *faith,* not proof. Of course, the changed life of the follower of Christ is the proof of his faith to himself and sometimes to others around him.

"So-Called" progressive creation

Mark D. Rasche of ICR (*Institute for Creation Research*, June 2003) says,

> "The **compromise of choice** today is known as *Progressive Creation*, a modern revision of the Day-Age Theory, advocating that the six days of creation can be equated with the billions of years of geology and astronomy; it proposes that God's creative acts occurred on widely separate occasions over the ages."

Of course, the terms in Genesis, *"Second day...third day; morning and evening"* refute such humanistic fanaticizing. The Bible teaches that the time will come when men will not endure sound doctrine and his itching ears will turn him away from the truth to follow **false teachers** and **fables.**

> *2 Timothy 4:3-4: For the time will come when **they will not endure sound doctrine**; but after their own lusts shall they heap to themselves teachers, having itching ears; And they shall turn away their ears from the truth, and shall be **turned unto fables**.*

Is there life on other planets?

Our government (USA) has foolishly spent many millions of dollars on outer space exploration in hopes of discovering the origin of human life and the universe. It is a sad fact that many scientists make no attempt to communicate with the God of creation through the Bible concerning origins and future life. However, they do strive to communicate with some form of alien/human life in outer space that does not even exist. As previously stated, the Bible plainly declares "Adam" to be the **first man** (I Corinthians 15:45) and his wife, Eve, the **mother of all living** (Genesis 3:20). The Scriptures are silent about any other *terrestrial* (earthly) being upon any other planet; however, the Scriptures do teach that the earth is uniquely the abode of man.

> *Psalms 115:16: The heaven, even the heavens, are the LORD'S: but **the earth hath he given to the children of men.***

> *Acts 17:26: And hath made of one blood **all nations of men for to dwell on all the face of the earth,** and hath determined the times before appointed, and the bounds of their habitation.*

Adam and Eve are the parents of all humans. You have it from the Word of God. You are either exercising your faith in the Bible record of beginnings or you are putting your faith in spurious conjectures of secular humanists.

If there is any form of life out there on other planets, it is relegated to celestial life such as angels (good angels or bad angels), not terrestrial life. The writer concedes the possibility that some UFO sightings may be related to the "chariots of God" and "angels" mentioned in the Bible (II Kings 2:11; 6:17; I Chronicles 28:18; Psalms 68:17; 104:3; Isaiah 66:15; Jeremiah 4:13). Although the writer believes that there *might* have been some genuine UFO celestial sightings, he puts little or no confidence in most UFO reports. It is indeed strange that UFOs have only reported to have been seen on earth, No UFOs have been reported in outer space and that too is strange considering that there are many telescopes around the world continually traversing the universe. Man appears to have an incurable desire to dare to be a witness to some great event.

Secular man insists that water, necessary to sustain human life, is out there in abundance in outer space in spite of evidence to the contrary (water is universally recognized by mankind as the solvent of life). Isn't it paradoxically strange that these same people who reject a worldwide flood in spite of well over half of the Earth's surface (two-thirds to three-fourths) being composed of water, cling to the claim of an abundance of water in outer space?

Ancient cities that were once above ground are now being discovered under the sea.

We could save a lot of taxpayer's money by simply believing God's Word.

(**NOTE:** Again, Creation has the opposite meaning of evolution. Creation is the instantaneous creation of matter from nothing by God. Phony evolution conjectures require millions of years, matter already created, victory over infinitesimal odds, a fantastic faith in nothingness, a warped world-view, hatred toward God's Word, a disengaged brain, and a very fat ego.

The deranged evolutionist believes that he is smarter than most folks.)

It is never too repetitious (superfluous; excessive; more than needed) to state that the main reason and by far the most important one for believing in **Creation** is because the Bible has declared it so. **GOD** created the heaven, the earth, and all things (Genesis 1:2; John 1:3, 10; Colossians 1:16-17; Ephesians 3:9; Hebrews 1:2). If we don't accept the Bible account of creation, obviously we are rejecting God's Word! This writer refuses to risk his soul upon the vain babblings of proud, finite men who are spouting platitudes about something they know not of.

Mankind in an unfair world

The writer suspects that the reason that some people passively assent to the teachings of evolution or atheism is because that an unfair world has dealt them a hard life; maybe they have been greatly mistreated and/or have had unjust and terrible things happen to them. Perhaps for this reason, they inwardly blame God and rebel at the Bible. However, the reason for the inequities in life cannot be blamed upon God but upon sin. Adam and Eve sinned first by disobedience in the Garden of Eden. We all inherited our sinful nature from our first parents. God knows all about heartbreak and inequity and sent His Son to die for sinners. The cure for sin has been paid for upon the Cross of Calvary and all man has to do is repent (change of mind and godly sorrow about sin, salvation and judgment) and receive (believe) God's payment (offering) for sin. Jesus died for the sins of the whole world (John 3:16)

The teaching of evolution in the public schools

In the United States, teachers do not have the freedom to teach the biblical account of Creation in the public schools. It is against the law! Of course, no one was there to observe Creation, so technically speaking, it was not an observable science...but neither has anyone observed a "so-called" evolution of beginnings. Evolution has had a total monopoly on education for decades. In general, evolutionist teachers in academia dare not allow openness or scientific accountability for fear they will lose their stranglehold. A "religion" of naturalism is being taught in the name of education. Of course, the complexity of life far exceeds the potential of natural processes.

There are double benefits for the evolutionists in the schools:

1) power over young minds   2) millions of dollars in textbooks.

Again, evolution, which was a strong influence on educator John Dewey, is just another false religion (among many others) that is based upon man's vain philosophy (Colossians 2:8; I Timothy 6:20). Its adherents worship creatures and makes nature and chance its god (Romans 1:25).

Sadly, it is rumored that even some private Christian schools are beginning to teach an 'old earth progressive creation' and an *allegorical* view of Genesis. They should honestly disclaim the name of Christian.

It was a sad day when our Federal Government got involved in public education. Our schools have degenerated both morally and scholastically ever since. Our national government has used the clever ploy of awarding tax money to those state schools willing to comply with federal guidelines and rulings of the court (of course, the tax money awarded to the schools originated from the states). It didn't take long for the federal government to outlaw the Bible and Christianity and establish evolution as the official religion in our schools.

It was also a sick note for America that it only took one man (Charles Darwin) and one woman (Madeline Murray O'Hare) to outlaw the Bible and Christianity and corrupt our schools. Of course, this would not have been possible without the concessions of political weaklings, carnal believers, dumbed-down educrats, and phony apostate religionists.

- Evolution dominates our national public school system

- Evolution re-creates man in the image of an ape (or monkey)

- Evolution downgrades Scripture into meaninglessness in most seminaries

- Evolution elicits personal attacks on creation by its supporters

It is really astounding to realize how easily our public schools and universities have been able to brainwash many of its students into believing that they have descended from apes or a particular line of monkeys (evolutionary hypotheses change so often, it's hard to keep up). Data from reliable sources say that evolution pseudo-science (voodoo-science) is rewritten about every 10 years. Apparently, some brainwashed students (certainly not all) either cannot or do not choose to think for themselves. Without a shred of tangible evidence and with a lot of *fuzzy logic* by brain-lame liberal professors, many have swallowed the preposterous world-view (philosophy) of evolution.

If it was a matter of who has the best mousetrap, this writer would not be too concerned, but when speaking of eternity, it is a completely different matter. The writer is certainly no "whiz kid," but he refuses to let ungodly egocentric man do his thinking for him. What could be more important than where and how we spend eternity?

Contrary to public education textbooks, the latest poll statistics (2002) say that a majority of Americans (about 83%) profess to believe in Creation (the writer believed in Creation before he was saved). As time elapses and evolutionists continue to control the education system of America, the percentage of believers in Creation will undoubtedly dwindle. The last report this writer came across (2010) was 53 percent belief of Americans in Creation. Even so, this writer puts little confidence in polls.

44

The opening of the door to evolution in our nation

Several things are significant to public education's molestation by ungodly humanism.

For one thing, preachers, Christians, and politicians all alike have stood by and done nothing to suppress the onslaught against our Christian heritage. **Edmund Burke** (1729-1797), an Irish statesman, author, political theorist, and philosopher, said, "All that is necessary for the triumph of evil is that good men do nothing."

One reliable source says,

> "Probably the great turning point in public education happened in 1947 when U.S. Supreme Court Justice, **Hugo Black**, lifted out of context part of a letter that **President Thomas Jefferson** wrote to the *Danbury Baptist Association* in 1801. Justice Black used this letter in the case of *Everson v. Board of Education* to fabricate the phony "wall of separation" between church and state. Black claimed that such a wall had to exist between church and state, completely ignoring Jefferson's true intent. Jefferson had meant that a wall had to exist to forbid the new government from intruding into the affairs of the Church."

It is clear that Jefferson did not mean that people in government could not freely express their religious belief in God and neither that God should be forbidden in our institutions. His intent was that the government should not sanction any particular

45

religious denomination (as in the union of state-church religions of European countries) nor prohibit anyone from expressing his religion. Black concluded that the reverse was also necessary, that the Church could not be involved with the affairs of the state. In our Constitution, there is absolutely no mention of the words, church, state, or separation. However, the First Amendment does guarantee the freedom of the expression of religion.

Amendment #1 of the Constitution: Congress shall make no law respecting an establishment of religion, **or prohibiting the free exercise thereof**; or abridging the freedom of speech, or of the press; or the right of the people peaceably to assemble, and to petition the government for a redress of grievances.

So why does our government now prohibit the speaking of Christ and His salvation within governmental realms? Our early American politicians and citizens alike knew how bigoted state-churches of Europe had bitterly persecuted minority Christian groups under the color of law during the Dark Ages (confiscating property; rape; torture; murder of about 50 million). Our earlier American history books taught us plainly that the main reason for Puritans, Pilgrims, Anabaptists, and others of like faith coming to the shores of America was to escape religious persecutions in Europe and to worship freely in the New World (our history books have since been rewritten and this fact of religious persecutions has been greatly covered up or cleverly eliminated). Has the reader no knowledge of *The Dark/Middle/Medieval Ages, The Spanish quisitions; The European Inquisitions; The Protestant Reformation; Fox's Book of Martyrs; Trail of the Blood; History of the Anabaptists?*

The design of early American politicians was to give us an Anglican or Episcopalian state-religion. Of course, taxpayers would have been forced to support this religion even if they disagreed with its creeds or doctrines.

(**Note:** Left-wing liberals and biased historians promote the lie that the majority of early American settlers only came to America for financial prosperity; the liberals purposely ignore the true fact that the settlers came to America to escape religious persecution in Europe. Of course, there were those that sought wealth among the early American settlers. Judas was the treasurer for the small band of apostles and he sold the Lord for a few pieces of silver.)

It appears that some of the Supreme Court Justices need to attend grade school to learn simple word definitions. **Amendment # 1** plainly says that government cannot favor or sanction a particular religious denomination **nor prohibit the citizen's right to freely exercise his religion**. Speaking of God and the Bible is not the same as endorsing a particular religious denomination such as Presbyterian, Methodist, Episcopalian, Lutheran, or any other Christian group. Orthodox denominations worship the same God of the same Bible. Since heathen promoters and sympathizers of evolution hold power in public education over the creationists, we have the answer to why evolution is taught in public education and why Christianity is opposed. Pagans now wear suits and ties!

Evolution: fact; theory; hypothesis; philosophy?

The reader may have observed that the writer has referred to evolution as a hypothesis or philosophy instead of a theory. The reason being is that evolution is far less than a theory simply because there is no evidence to qualify it at that level. Even a *hypothesis,* which a theory is based upon, does too much honor for evolution.

Dr. John D. Morris said,

> "Evolution is, therefore, neither fact, theory nor hypothesis. It is a belief---and nothing more" (*Acts and Facts*, February 2010, p. 17).

Evolution is a dung-hill philosophy of secular invention which makes man his own *little god.* Evolution is no more than *roguish* (dishonest; unscrupulous; rascal) science.

An atheist can spot phony religion

Atheist and vehement anti-creationist Dr. Eugenie Scott, in a magazine interview, once stated:

> "I have found that the most effective allies for evolution are people of the faith community. One clergyman with a backward collar is worth two biologists at a school board meeting any day!" (*The Voice in the Wilderness*, p.14, Asheville, NC, June 2005).

The writer readily admits that Dr. Scott speaks correctly for the apostate church community, but she definitely does not represent traditional Bible-believing Christian fundamentalism. The writer is proud to wear the badge of 'Bible fundamentalist" and offers no apology for his stand with the Bible.

(**Bible fundamentalism:** can be described simply as believing the basic or cardinal {of main importance; principal; chief} doctrines of the Scriptures. Examples: God Inspired and God Preserved Infallible Scriptures; First and Second Comings of Christ to Earth; Virgin Birth of Christ and His Deity; Trilogy of the Godhead, God the Father, God the Son, and God the Holy Spirit; a literal Heaven and Hell; all men are born sinners, and all men need the New Birth; Resurrection of Christ from the dead in a body; Resurrection of all to Eternal Life or to Eternal Damnation; Belief in Jesus Christ as the only way to Heaven; Creation of the universe by God in six literal 24/hour days. Of course, there are other fundamentally important doctrines besides these basics.)

An infidel's worst fear

An infidel said, "There is one thing that mars all the pleasures of my life."

"Indeed!" replied his friend. "What is that?"

He answered, "I am afraid the Bible is true. If I could know for certain that death is an eternal sleep, I should be happy; my joy would be complete! But here is the thorn that stings me. This is the word that pierces my very soul—if the Bible is true, I am lost forever!"

Is evolution 'science' and creation 'religion?'

The courts have declared evolution to be science and creation to be religion, and that religion doesn't belong in the public classroom. Intolerant "un-civil liberties" organizations such as **ACLU** ("so-called" American Civil Liberties Union) promise a lawsuit to anyone who would cross the unofficial line. There are many evolutionary claims in textbooks that are known to be false. Evolutionists will have it only their way.

(**Note:** The Special House Committee to investigate communist activities concluded: "The American Civil Liberties Union **{ACLU}** is closely affiliated with the communist movement in the United States, and fully ninety percent of its efforts are on behalf of communists who have come into conflict with the law." Of course, the main player {defending evolution} in the *Scope's Monkey Trial* of Dayton, Tennessee, was the ACLU.

The **ACLU** was formed in the 1920s primarily by two individuals, Crystal Eastman and Roger Baldwin. Roger Baldwin wrote, "I am for socialism {communism}, disarmament...the abolishing of the state itself...the abolition of the propertied class, and ...wealth.")

The writer wonders why politicians and the news media (local and national) will not speak out against un-American (or anti-American) organizations such as the ACLU and many other known organizations with evil designs against America. The national news channels are little more than 'news-propaganda machines' intent upon governing the minds of the un-suspecting populace. Many journalists are in fear of losing their jobs if they speak the whole truth; others are part of the problem and are walking in lock-step with the left-wing powers that be. The writer believes that most politicians, journalists, and national news media personnel are spineless stooges "singing for their supper."

Furthermore, this writer is suspicious of any organization that uses the words *American, People's, Freedom, or Progressive* in its title. Most of the time, these are "front-words" for socialist and communist groups that are anti-American and dedicated to the destruction of America. These harmless sounding titles are used as a ploy to deceive the naïve masses. Wake up America!

"So-called" evolution science does not qualify as true science

Actually, evolutionary science (advocating "origins" of kinds) is no more than voodoo science. The evidences, missing links, and bones of contention are nowhere to be found.

As previously stated, the very **Rules of Science** disqualify the ridiculous "so-called" theory of evolution. In other words, the *so-called* "science of evolution" is easily refuted by "The Laws of Science."

The Scientific Method demands at least three qualifications for a model or system to be established as a theory:

1.) Observation

2.) Experimentation

51

3.) Repetition (repeatability)

➢ No one has ever **observed** evolution occurring.

➢ No one has **experimented** with evolution.

➢ No one has ever **reproduced** (repeated) evolution.

A scientific theory must be based upon *repeatable observations* and subject to scientific investigation and tests. There were no observers to the origin of the universe (neither by creationists nor evolutionists).

The notion that "Creation is religion" has come about because most religions are anemic or plain phony. There is only ONE true religion and that is the one of Bible faith in God's Only Begotten Son, Jesus Christ, the Righteous.

Others that once acknowledged Creation have long since become apostate and have departed from the truth of Biblical Creation. Of course, true believers acknowledge Bible Creation and refute evolution (of origins). True science acknowledges Creation and false science honors evolution.

(**Evolution:** nothing appeared out of nowhere and evolved into green murky gases, complex amino acids, amoebas/hydras (unicellular animals}, multi-cellular animals, monkeys, monkey's descendants, college professors, unbiased evolutionists.)

Gravity is not evolution

Some claim that "gravity" is evolution; however, the effects of gravity can be *observed,* _erimented, and repeated_. Gravity is true science, ,ot a dummy hodgepodge science. Gravity is more than a theory; it is a law and has never been known to fail. Though we may temporarily overcome gravity (airplanes; rockets; balloons; et al), gravity still remains.

Again, evolution does not even qualify to be labeled a _hypothesis_ (which a theory is based upon). Let's try _psycho-babbling_ or _evil-lution_. Again, according to scientific rules, evolution does not qualify as science.

(**Note:** The original etymology of the word _evolution_ had the basic meaning of _change,_ not _origin. Webster's Ninth New Collegiate Dictionary_ defines evolution as-_n_ [L evolution-, evolutio unrolling, fr. evolutus, pp. of evolvere] (1622). **A process of change in a certain direction**. _The American Dictionary of the English Language-Noah Webster-1828_ defines evolution as simply unrolling or unfolding, not an origin.)

The mature Christian community acknowledges **changes** within kinds but glorifies God in **origins** (beginnings) of kinds.

Mutations do not support evolution

Evolutionists teach that mutations can make a new, improved creature and that _natural selection_ helps it survive and take over the population. In his video, _Lies In The Textbook,_ **Dr. Hovind** says:

> "Mutations do happen but they are always either fatal, harmful, or neutral. No mutation has ever been observed that improved on the original. They are accidents to the original

come forth from inorganic sludge; live cells do not develop from dead matter and slime.

Dr. John Moore spoke during the annual sessions of the American Association for the Advancement of Science. He described the theory that man evolved from "amoeba and sea-slimes" as an "incredible religion," but not "science."

Neither did we evolve from pond-scum! This writer is wary of those who espouse such foolery.

The Primordial Law of the Universe is *natura semper scalas descendet*, nature always descends, that is, *devolves*. Therefore, devolution, never evolution, is the relentless, inescapable law of the universe (Mastropaolo, Joseph, *The Rise and Fall of Evolution, A Scientific Examination*, 2003, pp. 115-123).

Evolution is no more than and no less than warmed over pagan superstition revived over the coals of unbelief.

2.) Like always gives rise to like-kind (or, like-things produce like-things).

This is commonly referred to as "Biogenesis."

Nobody has ever observed and intermediate step of one kind of "life form" change to "another kind of life form."

Evolution of origins and Creation cannot really co-exist because Creation (origins) deals with truth and evolution (origins) deals with preposterous lies.

Both the *"First and Second Laws of Thermodynamics"* refute evolution as a proven fact.

No exception to the two laws of thermodynamics has ever been found.

The Second Law of Thermodynamics (The Law of Entropy S) discounts evolution. **The Law of Entropy S** says that any system left to itself (isolated or open systems) tends to decrease in organized complexity and increases toward randomness (disorder). In other words, the system or organism eventually breaks down into its simplest elements. When a dead body begins its decaying process, the resultant is carbon dioxide, carbolic acid, water, et al. It does not build up into a more complex form. The Law of Entropy S assures us that everything decays and dies.

The Bible tells us that the present earth and heaven "shall wax old as doth a garment" and "shall perish" (Hebrews 1:11; I John 2:17).

It is absurd to think that the cosmos could have "organized" itself by the same processes that are "disorganizing" it (The Law of Entropy S). However, evolutionists continue on to delude themselves into believing this of a highly complex and energized universe.

(**Note:** *Horizontal* variations and *downward* mutations are accepted by both creationists and evolutionists. However, there is not one proof of an *upward* evolution. There are millions of fossils in the rocks and none show an upwards transitional form or intermediate step to bridge one basic kind to another basic kind. The millions of basic fossil kinds would demand, at least, many billions of transitional forms if evolution had legs to stand on.)

56

This writer asked his college chemistry professor (1974) his view on **Entropy S** (true science) versus evolution (false science). The only part of the professor's answer that was understood by this writer was, "You have to consider." It was never clear what mechanisms I had to consider! My professor was an excellent chemistry teacher, but his answer to my question was quite inadequate and evasive. The professor's answer to any baffling question involving chemistry was to always claim "resonance." The eureka (cure-all; panacea; voila!) for the unanswerable problems of life and chemistry was to claim 'chemical resonance.' A reasonable answer from the well-liked and capable professor was not forthcoming.

Miracles rejected by naturalists

Higher critics and naturalists reject *supernaturalism* on scientific grounds alone. The truth is that *naturalism* **cannot account for the known facts**. Pseudo-science insists that naturalism must govern all phenomena and that real miracles (the supernatural) are impossible. Of course, the question is not "could a miracle happen?" but "did the miracle happen?"

In *Acts and Facts* (November 2009, p. 18), David Coppedge says:

> "Actually, miracles are quite rampant in the evolutionary story. The literature of biological evolution is replete with statements that this or that animal evolved whatever complex systems are needed along the way, as if it makes it so. Examples of miracles in evolutionary philosophy include the sudden appearance of

the universe without cause or explanation, the origin of life, the origin of sex, the origin of animal and plant body plans, and the origin of human consciousness. The evolutionist's Big Bang theory certainly involves a miracle! Naturalists (who say nature is all there is) believe they can invent explanations that are free of miracles, but in practice, **miracles pop us everywhere in their stories**."

In answer to both miraculous creation and the supernatural claims of evolutionists, the writer is compelled to say, "Duh; everybody believes in miracles, don't they?"

Coppedge quotes Finagle's 6th Rule of Science: "Do not believe in miracles, Rely on them."

Creation and resurrection are the greatest miracles in all of history. Without miracles, there would not have been the 'creation of the world.' Without miracles, there would have been no 'resurrection' of its Creator, Jesus Christ, from physical death. Without **creation** we would have no existence and without **resurrection** we would have no hope of life after death.

The Apostle Paul of the New Testament answered King Agrippa's skepticism concerning Christ's resurrection saying, "Why should it be thought a thing incredible with you, that God should raise the dead?" (Acts 26:8).

Evolution is simply another gigantic hoax (or "frenzied fantasy") of unbelievers. Evolution is no more than "bogus" science or a "crutch" to prop up its fable. The writer sees little difference between the inane and absurd fables of Greek mythology and evolution philosophy; both have false gods.

Evolutionists try to explain the contemporary by fantastic or supernatural leaps of faith (a fish into an amphibian; a dinosaur into a bird; an ape into a man).

On a grand scale, evolution implies a common ancestry of all life, including molecule-to-amoeba-to-monkey-to-man. We definitely have a common ancestry but not according to murky evolution. Our common ancestry began with Adam and Eve and proceeded from the sons of Noah after the Genesis flood. It's all in the Bible!

Variance in reproductions

If evolution had legs to stand on, all forms of life could now mingle and reproduce sexually or asexually (budding; fission; et al). There would be no limit upon reproduction of various seeds germinating various eggs. According to evolutionists, the longer ages explain everything and make all things possible (inanimate matter to unicellular life to monkey flesh to human flesh). If we are millions of years beyond the "so-called" evolution of beginnings, why do animals and plants die? Why isn't evolution easily observable, workable, and provable than ever before? There are no proofs of evolution occurring today! If evolution has stopped, why did it stop? If evolution has a bone of contention, it should be extremely evident after establishing itself for millions of years! And yet, there is not one single tangible proof to prop up the evolutionist's dream. The Bible has had the answer all along.

Does animal flesh evolve into human flesh?

Human flesh does not evolve from animal flesh. There is a chasm that cannot be bridged between different **kinds** of flesh. Everything reproduces "after his kind" (Genesis 1:24, 25).

> *I Corinthians 15:39-44:* **All flesh is not the same flesh**: *but there is one kind of* **flesh of men**, *another* **flesh of beasts**, **another of fishes**, *and* **another of birds**. *There are also celestial bodies, and bodies terrestrial: but the glory of the celestial is one, and the glory of the terrestrial is another. There is one glory of the sun, and another glory of the moon, and another glory of the stars: for one star differeth from another star in glory. So also is the resurrection of the dead. It is sown in corruption; it is raised in incorruption: It is sown in dishonour; it is raised in glory: it is sown in weakness; it is raised in power: It is sown a natural body; it is raised a spiritual body. There is* **a natural body**, *and there is* **a spiritual body**.

The first part of the above text in First Corinthians makes it clear that human flesh and beast flesh are different. Human flesh does not evolve from beast (animal) flesh as evolutionists claim (amoeba-fish-bird-monkey-man). The writer questions the rationality of people who believe that they evolved from a particle of dust, an amino acid, primordial soup, unicellular animal, and ultimately

60

from a chimp (beast flesh). It appears to this writer that the people that have come from the monkeys have gone back to the dogs!

Our God is a miracle working God who created man in one day. God did not need millions of years and numerous stages of development of man-flesh from animal flesh.

The writer is sure that he has discovered the biblical reason of why "so-called" intelligent secularists are so easily deceived concerning the false premise of the evolutionist of beginnings:

> 2 Corinthians 4:4: In whom the god of this world (Satan) hath blinded the minds of them which believe not, lest the light of the glorious gospel of Christ, who is the image of God, should shine unto them.

When men go so far as to disbelieve or discredit the Bible, God may turn them over to Satan and to a reprobate mind that they may be damned forever.

> 2 Thessalonians 2:11, 12: And for this cause God shall send them **strong delusion**, that they should **believe a lie**: That they all might **be damned** who believed not the truth, but had pleasure in unrighteousness.

These verses above are in reference to the near approaching Day of Christ (for true believers) and the near approaching Day of the LORD (for unbelievers). In this apostasy that occurs in the latter days right before the First Resurrection (rapture) and the beginning of Daniels's Seventh Week of Prophecy (Daniel 9:24-27), God will turn the minds of unbelieving men over to Satan with all power and signs and lying wonders. Those who have heard the truth of the Gospel and trodden it under foot, will never have another chance for salvation and will not only have to endure the horrible atrocities of the Great Tribulation upon earth, but will also be cast into the Lake of Fire to suffer forever. Unbelievers will be without a sacrificial Saviour and they will stand bare before God having their eternal destiny fixed without a glimmer of hope. They had known the truth of God's love and forgiveness and in their foolish pride, rejected it.

God did all the work that is needed for man's salvation when He sent His Son to die upon Calvary's Cross. All man has to do is receive God's sacrificial offering for sin, Jesus Christ.

> *Revelation 20:14, 15: And death and hell were cast into the **lake of fire**. This is the second death. And whosoever was not found written in the book of life was cast into the **lake of fire**.*

Of course, the atheist and evolutionist may say, "I don't believe in a Hell or place of torment." Unbelief doesn't change God's Word one iota (Romans 3:3).

Secular intelligence vs. common sense

The writer recalls a situatiion in the 1950's during his Army stint while stationed at Fort Carson, Colorado (formerly Camp Kit Carson) near Colorado Springs. There was a soldier in our headquarters company that had a high IQ ('intelligence quotient') but had very little common sense. The writer, having access to personnel files (Military 201 Jackets),

62

looked up the soldier's military file and verified his high IQ score. The likable soldier's high IQ combined with his lack of common sense (which was exhibited daily) made for a friendly joke to all the GIs. The reader may rightfully question the point of this story! The moral of the story is simply that intellectual, secular or scholastic intelligence alone is not a sure guide to truth (especially that of a spiritual nature). A rocket scientist may believe in evolution but his high carnal intelligence is no proof of its veracity (just as the soldier's high IQ was no proof that he had true intelligence (common sense). Besides, there are many educated and intelligent people who believe in Creation. All true intelligent people do not belong to the caste of "monkey see, monkey do." There are highly intelligent people who can think for themselves (outside the secular box):

People with common sense (which is superior to intellectual evolutionary-intelligence) acknowledge that the heavens declare the glory of God (Psalms 19:1-3).

The writer proposes a simple question: who is the *wiser* of the two following persons?

a.) A highly educated scientific person that is convinced of **evolution of origins**

b.) An uneducated illiterate pipe-smoking grandmother with enough common sense to believe in **Biblical Creation of origins.**

The writer has no problem in selecting grandmother as far wiser than the educated pagan evolutionist (pagans wear suits and ties as well as loin cloths and beads of animal teeth). This writer is

63

thankful that rocket-science intelligence is not required to exercise faith in God's Word (else this writer would be left out). The wisdom of common sense far exceeds *the contemporary wisdom of this world* (I Corinthians 1:18-21). There is no excuse for rejecting truth as revealed in the Bible just because there is a caste of educated humanists (ego maniacs) and secular educators that support the foolishness of evolution. Most famed, wealthy, and educated people are too proud to condescend to the low estate of the common person who puts their faith in God. Of course, the wisest man (though an imperfect sinner) that ever lived believed in God. His name was Solomon.

> *I Corinthians 1:26-28: For ye see your calling, brethren, how that **not many wise men after the flesh**, **not many mighty not many noble**, are called. But God hath chosen the foolish things of the world to confound the wise: and God hath chosen the weak things of the world to confound the things which are mighty; And base things of the world, and, things which are despised, hath God chosen, yea and things which are not, to bring to nought things that are.*

God will not call sinners to salvation when they resist the truth of His Word.

> *Psalms 19:1: The heavens declare the glory of God; and the firmament sheweth his handywork*

Neither evolution nor Creation can be scientifically proven. The decision ultimately boils down to what or to whom one places their faith.

Creationists versus evolutionists

Most secular scientists imply that all founding fathers of science have believed in evolution and do not believe in *creation, resurrection, or miracles*. However, evolution is not *warm and fuzzy* as the Darwinians would have you believe. About 10,000 scientists in the USA and about 100,000 creation scientists in the world reject Darwinism and hold a creation worldview (The secular elements of this ungodly world only promote their own kind and care not for those that honor God's record in the Bible). The evolution infidels pretend that great minds of the world were arrayed against Jesus Christ and the Church. If you ask them to name the great men of evolution, they will name Darwin, Huxley, Spencer, Voltaire, Ingersoll the agnostic, Sagan, and a few others (of course, of late, public education has now produced many more "monkey fans"). Factually, practically all the great minds of the world believed in Creation and the same holds true for today.

Robert Dick Wilson, Professor of Semite Philology of Princeton University, could teach 26 languages and read 45. He was an astute astronomer and knew most of the sciences. Mr. Wilson believed, "In the beginning God created the heaven and the earth" and that "God created man in his own image" (Genesis 1:1, 27). --(*The Sword of the Lord*, June 6, 2003, p. 8).

Don't expect the evolutionists to mention the following creationist scientists and great minds:

Galileo; Louis Agassiz (Glacial Geology; Ichthyology);

Isaac Newton (Calculus/ Dynamics/ Law of Gravity/Reflecting Telescope);

Francis Bacon (Scientific Method);

Robert Boyle (Chemistry; Gas Dynamics);

Georges Cuvier (Comparative Anatomy/ Vertebrate Paleontology);

Blaise Pascal (Hydrostatics; Barometer);

Michael Faraday (Electromagnetics; Field Theory; Electric Generator);

Joseph Henry (Electric Motor/Self-induction/Galvanometer);

John Ambrose Flemming (Electronics);

William Herschel (Double Stars);

James Joule (Reversible Thermodynamics);

Carolus Linnaeus (Systemtic Biology/Animal Classification Nomenclature);

Joseph Lister (Antiseptic Surgery);

James Maxwell; Gregor Mendel (Genetics);

Louis Pasteur (Bacteriology/Vaccination and Immunization/Biogenesis Law/Fermentation Control/ Pasteurization);

Lord Raleigh (Model Analysis);

Johannes Kepler (Celestial Mechanics/ Physical Astronomy/Ephemeris Tables);

Ray, Lord Kelvin (Transatlantic Cable/Energetics/Thermodynamics, Absolute Temperature Scale);

Adams; George Bullen; Watts (Steam Engine);

Fulton (Steamboat);

McCormick (Reaper);

Samuel F.B. Morse (Telegraph);

Whitney (Cotton Gin);

Charles Babbage (Computer Science/Actuarial Tables/Calculating Machine);

Lord Rayleigh (Dimensional Analysis);

James Clerk Maxwell (Statistical Thermodynamics; Electrodynamics);

Harvey (physician who discovered circulation of the blood);

Henri Fabre (Entomology of Living Insects);

George Stokes (Fluid Mechanics);

William Herschel (Galactic Astronomy);

James Simpson (Gynecology/Chloroform);

Leonardo da Vinci (Hydraulics);

Matthew Maury (Hydrography; Oceanography);

William Ramsay (Isotopic Chemistry/Inert Gases);

John Ray (Natural History);

Bernharad Riemann (Non-Euclidean Geometry);

David Brewster (Optical Mineralogy);

John Woodward (Paleontology);

Rudolph Virchow (Pathology);

Nicholas Steno (Stratigraphy);

Humphry Davy ((Thermokinetics/Mine Safety Lamp);

John Herschel (Global Star Catalog);

Ambrose Fleming (Thermionic Valve); and thousands of today's creation scientists).

Of course, many others (poets; statesmen; artists; philosophers) believed in the great Creator God:

Tennyson, **Longfellow;** Leonardo **da Vinci**, **Murillo; Reuben; Whittier; Garfield;** William **McKinley;** John **Hay;** Theodore **Roosevelt; Bryan; Wilson; Hughes;** Champ **Clark; Burke** (Statesman); **Byron** (Statesman); **Bacon** (philosopher); **Raphael** (the painter); **Michelangelo** (sculptor); **Milton** (Paradise Lost); **Dante** (Dante's Inferno).

The writer is not stating that all of these men were born again believers, but he is saying that they believed the Bible and in Creation, not evolution.

The American educator and journalist, **Noah Webster** (of the famed *Webster Dictionary*) said that a man is not adequately educated unless he was learned in the Bible.

Mr. Webster was one of the most educated men of America (qualified authorities say he was the most educated man that America ever produced).

William Jennings Bryan wrote about evolution, "millions of guesses strung together."

Creation is expressly stated in the book of Genesis and many other places in Scriptures.

Peter W. Stoner lists thirteen steps of creation as recorded in Genesis, Chapter 1 of the Bible, and comes to the conclusion that these events are not only accurately recorded, but are in an order

68

acceptable to modern science. He estimates (as a mathematician) that Moses' chance of getting both the items and order correct, without Divine aid, are, "one in 31, 135, 103, 000, 000, 000, 000, 000" or, one in 31 sextillion 135 quintillion 103 quadrillion (*The Biblical Evangelist*, Nov-Dec, 2004, p 13).

Chief judge of the Georgia Court of Appeals, **Braswell Deen**, referring to the evolutionary hypothesis, said, "I call it the Mickey Mouse Mentality Monkey Mythology, Methodology Monopoly, Mysterious Musings and Mundane Dreams of All This Monkey Business" *(The Sword of the Lord,* June 6, *2003, p. 8).*

Evolution is so popularly touted in public academia that one would hardly suspect that there are rational people who only accept the Bible account of Creation.

The writer (ddh) says about evolution, "Evolution fantasies are the dreams of prideful, self-sufficient humanists trying to express themselves intellectually but instead as fools."

Psalms 14:1 verifies this foolishness of man.

Mr. William Shakespeare (April 23, 1564 - April 23, 1616), the greatest playwright the world has ever known, after writing 37 plays, wrote:

> "I commend my soul into the hands of God, my **Creator**, hoping and assuredly believing, **through the only merits of Jesus Christ, my Saviour**, to be made partaker of life everlasting."

The careers (and salaries) of evolutionist scientists are riding upon Darwinism. Evolution actually belongs to "Bubbleland" with Snow White and the Seven Dwarfs. God even *created* Darwin (without his infidelity: that was acquired).

In the whole of humanity, Bible believers have always been in the minority. Of course, scientific truth is established by scientific facts, not by majority vote of atheists, Bible deniers, and evolutionists.

What about the Age of dinosaurs?

Dinosaurs are the same age as man (Genesis 1:21, 24, 25), regardless of the totally unsubstantiated hypothesis of Darwinism that is entrenched in science and education (as the only acceptable view).

Dr. Shelton Smith (editor of *The Sword of the Lord*) says,

> *(1)* Darwinism is scientifically flawed and inherently weak. It survives well where it has a monopoly and there is no competition. Strange, isn't it, that the free discussion of ideas is stifled on this in a "free speech" society?

> (2) Darwinism poses as science when in reality it is its religious values that propel it. If it gives creation credibility, that means admitting there is a God in Heaven who is the Creator. That is one problem Darwinists refuse to address. After all, if there is indeed a Creator God, He just might have some other ideas on some other subjects that would put a crimp in their lifestyle.

Ken Ham says,

"Unfortunately, most people equate dinosaurs with millions of years and the evolution belief system. Dinosaurs have become almost icons for evolutionary teaching – they're treated as sacred 'gods' that belong only to evolutionist for their purpose of indoctrinating generations in secular humanism."

Dr. David Catchpoole states:

"A recent New Scientist article ponders an enigma to evolutionist – 'living fossils.' These are creatures alive today which are identical to fossilized forms, believed to have lived 'millions of years ago.' Examples include the coelacanth fish (fossil coelacanths are believed by evolutionists to be 340 million years old), Gingko trees (125 million years), crocodiles (140 million years)..."

All of these live today beside humans, and yet according to evolutionists, date back to before or at the time of the dinosaurs.

Why then would it be so ridiculous to think that dinosaurs also lived beside humans but have died out in recent times? It is not ridiculous to believe dinosaurs and humans lived at the same time.

ICR (*Institute for Creation Research*) states,

"Hailed in 1953 as "the most important zoological discovery of this century," a rather strange looking fish had been caught off the coast of Madagascar. This five-foot, 100-pound creature had been missing for 75 million years! Evolutionary scientist had used the fossil remains of *Coelacanth* as evidence for the evolution of fish to amphibians, and were, needless to say, somewhat surprised to find this "extinct" animal alive and well in the Indian Ocean (**ICR**, *Acts & Facts*, Vol. 32, No. 4, p. 7, April 2003, P.O. Box 2667, El Cajon, CA 92021).

Kenneth Ham (president of *Answers in Genesis*) says,

> "The recent discovery of a dinosaur bone in Montana supports the biblical creationist view of a young Earth." In 2003, a research team found a tyrannosaurus rex thighbone during an archaeological dig. The research team had to break the bone in pieces in order to fit it into a helicopter, and when they did so, they discovered the fossil contained well-preserved soft tissue including flexible blood vessels. "You would not expect soft tissue and cells like this in a bone supposedly 70 million years old."

The general consensus among scientists prior to the find was that such soft tissue could not survive for tens of millions of years. Creationist scientists would say that these bones aren't that old and probably date back to the time of the Flood just a few thousand years ago. Nothing has been found to contradict biblical creation but over and over much is found that contradicts evolution. Evolutionists will say anything rather than admit to Biblical Creation.

It appears that almost everyone, from small children to senior citizens, is fascinated with dinosaurs. Some even go so far as to discredit the Bible because they cannot find a dinosaur in it.

The writer believes that dinosaurs are in the Bible but not by that name. The word *dinosaur* and similar other names are of **recent invention (**such as "homosexual**)**. The King James Bible was translated over 200 years before dinosaur remains were found and given a name.

(**Note:** Neither will you find a pig or hog in the Bible by that name; you would have to refer to *swine*. Neither will *y*ou find any animals in the Bible; there are only *beasts*.)

Secular science claims that dinosaurs lived upon the earth 200 million years ago. Then about 65 million years ago they died out rather suddenly (*World Book Ency.*, Volume 5, p. 170, Copyright 1980).

The writer believes that the extinction of the dinosaurs was due to a harsh earth environment resulting from Noah's Flood. The flood, which lasted over one year, severely limited the food source for the dinosaurs; hence the devastated earth could not produce sufficient food rapidly enough to sustain the massive animals (my opinion).

Dinosaur fossils have been discovered with attached soft flesh, implying a young age. The writer does not believe that soft flesh could survive millions or billions of years without fossilizing or disintegrating.

If the reader believes God's infallible Word, you know that dinosaurs are no older than any other animal or beast of the earth (Genesis 1:24). Again, the dinosaur is the same age as Adam, the first man (Genesis 1:24-31). They both were created on the

6th day. That makes both man and dinosaur less than 10,000 years old (again, the writer believes both to be *about* 6,000 years old).

(**Note:** The writer believes that dinosaurs are mentioned in the Bible, even if not by their contemporary assortment of names. The **behemoth** and **leviathan** of Job 40 and 41 are certainly good candidates for dinosaurs. The writer believes that the behemoth is in reference to the dinosaur. For more on the subject of dinosaurs, the reader may refer to the writer's paper, *Are Dinosaurs in the Bible?*)

In contrast to the value of a man's soul, dinosaurs do not measure one whit of importance, and the Bible has much to say about that (Matthew 10:28; 16:26; Mark 8:36, 37).

Three Forms of Life on Earth

It needs to be acknowledged that animals (called beasts in the Bible) do not have a spirit that would enable them to worship God (no apology to animal ancestor worshippers!).

♦ **Plant life:** has only has a body (Greek: *soma*). It has no soul (self-conscious life) nor spirit to seek God.

♦ **Animal life:** has a body (Greek: *soma*) and also a soul (Greek: *psyche*) enabling it to have self-conscious life. However, animals were not made in the image of God and do not possess a spirit (*pneuma*) that would enable them to seek to worship God.

> *John 4:24: God is a Spirit: and they that worship him must worship him in spirit and in truth.*

♦ **Man:** is the crown of God's creation (Hebrews 2:6). According to I Thessalonians 5:23, man has body (Greek: *soma*), soul (Greek: *psyche*), and spirit (Greek: *pneuma*). The spirit of man drives him to worship. Man is incurably religious. If man does not worship the one and only true God, he will worship nature and creatures of his own fancy (as himself).

Man plagued by idolatry

Man (the highest form of terrestrial life and the crown of God's earthly creation) is guilty of at least two kinds of idolatry, worship of **heavenly bodies** and the worship phony deities through **images** and **idols,** both dead and alive.

Diana was the **moon goddess** of Rome (identified with Greek Artemis); Allah of Islam is the **moon god** of ancient Persia (Iran) and /or Arabia.

Bible writers say that the first form of idolatry of early man was the worship of the luminaries (sun, moon, stars, and constellations). We see this proof in Deuteronomy 4:19; 17:3.

It appears to the writer that the worship of false deities through the medium of images and icons is by far the leading form of idolatry.

A major religious cult (with about a billion followers) incorporates the practice of bowing before statues and images (even kissing some). Some kiss the pope's ring; others kiss the big toe of Peter's

75

statue (nearly eroding it away). These practitioners boldly break the First Commandment:

> *Exodus 20:3-5; Deuteronomy 5:7-9: Thou shalt have no other gods before me. Thou shalt not make unto thee **any graven image**, or **any likeness of any thing** that is in heaven above, or that is in the earth beneath, or that is in the water under the earth. **Thou shalt now bow down thyself to them**, nor serve them: for I the LORD thy God am a jealous God, visiting the iniquity of the fathers upon the children unto the third and four generation of them that hate me.*

(**NOTE:** Of course, today we live in societies that offer far more forms of idolatry than olden times. To mention a few, we have competitive sports, education, art, career vocations, money, entertainment, fishing, hunting, nature, et al. Within themselves, there is nothing wrong with these things, but anything that would come *between* a person and his appeal to God for salvation could be properly labeled an "idol." Too, if an unbeliever allows a church hypocrite to stand between himself and God, the unbeliever is merely a smaller hypocrite than the church hypocrite. At the Day of Judgment, no one will have to answer for other hypocrites, just for themselves. But that will be too late.)

Worship of the true God is not enhanced or facilitated by bowing down before images or statues, as points of contact, as was practiced by pagans. True worshippers of God worship Him in spirit and in truth (John 4:23, 24). The Scriptures in Exodus as well as many other books of the Bible clearly forbid the use of idolatrous images or "any likeness of any thing." This would include prayers to Mary (the "so-called" mediatrix) as well as prayers to "so-called" canonized saints (who some consider as mediators or go-betweens). There is only **ONE MEDIATOR** between God and men, the man, **Christ Jesus** (I Timothy 2:5: John 14:6; Acts 4:10-12).

Besides luminaries and many forms of false gods, the writer would like to inject another object of idolatry, the prideful, independent self-sufficient man himself. We call it "humanism."

Bible salvation versus humanistic evolution

Matthew 16:26: For what is a man profited, if he shall gain the whole world, and lose his own soul?

Atheism and evolution (close kin) have nothing to offer but eternal damnation. A wise person will prepare his soul in plenty of time before death and the Day of Judgment when God's wrath falls upon the ungodly. When the sinner's cup of iniquity is filled up (as in the case of Israel, pagan nations, and others), it is too late for repentance and turning around for God's mercy.

Jesus suffered the sinner's deserved judgment (Hell) upon the cross of Calvary. All ("whosoever will may come") can repent and freely receive Him as Lord and Saviour. By faith alone, any sinner has only to trust God's sacrifice for his sin (John 3:16, 18: Romans 10:13; 2 Peter 3:9; Revelation 22:17).

77

Neither is there any such thing as a purgatory, a limbo state, or a middle (neutral) ground after death that affords a second chance for salvation. When one passes the final outpost of life, death settles a man's eternal state.

Second Thessalonians Chapter 2 is quite clear concerning those who have ignored and scoffed at God's Word. It will be woe to them who have been presumptuous towards God's mercy. Scriptures sound a clear warning to those who would trust in a second chance for salvation after death.

We are only guaranteed today:

> 2 Corinthians 6:2: "...behold, **now** is the accepted time: behold, **now** is the day of salvation."

> Hebrews 2:3: "How shall we escape if we **neglect** so great salvation...".

> Hebrews 9:27: And as it is appointed unto men once to die but after this the **judgment**.

The Translation (Rapture) of the Church and the Beginning of Daniel's 70th Week of Prophecy

Some of the Bible references to the First Resurrection (translation) of the Church are: Titus 2:13; I Corinthians 15:51-58; I Thessalonians 4:13-18; Revelation 3:10; 4:1; I Thessalonians 5:9; Romans 5:9). This First Resurrection, or translation of the Church, is commonly referred to as "The Rapture."

Following soon after the translation of the Church, the Seven-Year Tribulation period begins:

> *2 Thessalonians 2:7-12: For the mystery of iniquity doth already work: only he now letteth will let, until he be taken out of the way. And **then** shall that Wicked be revealed, whom the Lord shall consume with the spirit of his mouth and shall destroy with the brightness of his coming: Even him, whose coming is after the working of Satan with all power and signs and lying wonders. And with all deceivableness of unrighteousness in them that perish; **because they received not the love of the truth**, that they might be saved. And for this cause **God shall send them strong delusion, that they should believe a lie: That they all might be damned who believed not the truth but had pleasure in unrighteousness.***

Romans 10:13: For **whosoever** shall call upon the name of the Lord shall be saved.

Evolution requires too much faith

The atheistic concept of evolution (origins; beginnings) should be classified as a primitive, and brutish "man-made" philosophy because there is no proof for it of any kind (especially scientific proof). If the reader stops to think about it, he will realize that the far out "wannabe" fantasies and dreams of evolutionists require much greater faith to believe in than does simple faith in Biblical Creation. Anyone who accepts evolution as a proven fact has been cleverly brainwashed by Darwinians and left-wing liberal professors; they have ceased to use common sense.

Both atheism and Darwinism are matters of *faith* (and so is Creation). There is no neutral

EVOLUTION: ANOTHER FALSE RELIGIION OF HUMANISM

position, you either believe God's Word or you don't! Evolution is certainly not scientific fact. It is secular humanism acknowledging a false "world-view" of the intelligent design of God's creation. Darwinians worship the creation rather than the Creator (Romans 1:25). Man, it appears, is incurably religious but has different gods

Intelligent Design

At a conference in 2009, Dr. James S. Johnson was asked by a Christian schoolteacher if he was part of the Intelligent Design Movement. Dr. Johnson replied, "No, I belong to the Intelligent Designer Movement. The teacher asked, "What's the difference?" "Jesus!" Dr. Johnson replied. The person of Jesus Christ is the pivotal difference between the **IDM** (Intelligent Design Movement) and Biblical creationism. IDM analyzes and describes the natural creation in a way that implies credit to an anonymous "someone." But a Biblical creationist is quick to actually identify nature's Designer as the God of the Bible. As a whole, there is little room for Jesus in the Intelligent Design Movement (though some acknowledge Him). There is certainly no room in IDM for God's inspired book, the Holy Bible. Dr. Johnson says that teaching about 'intelligent design' without identifying who designed it, is to be guilty of appreciating and glorifying the creation itself more than the Creator, which Paul rightly faults in Romans 1:23 (*Acts and Facts*, February 2010, p. 19).

Others refer to creation as "Divine Design" which does not give the proper glory to God. The singular emphasis on design shifts the attention to creation rather than to the Creator Himself. Nature worshippers are exposed in Romans 1:21-25.

(**Note:** Not all "Intelligent Design Movement" {IDM} people are creationists or even Christian.)

Evolution origins are: "ridiculous-incredulous-insane-preposterous-unbelievable."

Someone has well stated, "There is much more likelihood that tossing a bunch of scrap metal up into the air will fall to the ground formed into a Rolex watch than for evolution to take place."

- **George J. Romanes** said, "You can't explain this world upon any other hypothesis than God Almighty made it."

- **Sir George Cooker** said, "I know of no sound conclusions of science that are opposed to the Bible and the Christian religion."

- **Thomas Edison** said, "There is enough evidence in chemistry to prove the existence of God to say nothing about human experience."

- **Lord Calvin** said, "It is absurd to believe the atoms falling together of their own accord could make a sprig of grass, a rock, or living being."

- **Dr. J.O. Kinnaman** said, "Of the hundreds of thousands of artifacts found by the archaeologists, not one has ever been discovered that contradicts or denies one word, phrase, clause, or sentence of the Bible, but always confirms and verifies the facts of the biblical record" (*Sword of the Lord*, January 19, 2001, p.4).

• **Frank Sherwin** says, "Science has repeatedly shown the incredibly small chance of organic life arising from inorganic non-life (biogenesis)."

Mr. Sherwin adds, "The naturalist (*evolutionist*) has no choice, no recourse, but to place their faith in the infinitesimal odds that life just might spring from this sludge (a gooey tar on the walls of the reaction vessel)...They are betting their eternal destiny on chances that any odds master would see as much too slim to even consider."

• "...more than 40 years of work has failed to produce any convincing detailed scheme as to how living cells could have evolved from simple organic molecules" (Palmer, T. *Controversy: Catastrophism & Evolution*, Kluwer Academic, 1999, p. 264).

Again, why didn't all monkeys evolve into human beings? Why aren't some monkeys evolving into human beings now? Maybe some are de-evolving because there are claims that evolution has made monkeys out of the university professors!

Perhaps the reader thinks that this writer is unnecessarily harsh towards evolutionists and should not ridicule them. It is of the utmost importance to awaken the evolutionists to their great error and damnable trust in evolution, which is an insidious philosophy. The foolishness of disbelief in God's Word will damn a soul to Hell (Mark 9:43-48), not for a little while, but forever.

John 8:24: I (Jesus) said therefore unto you, that ye shall die in your sins: **for if ye believe not that I am he, ye shall die in your sins.**

Belief in evolution is in opposition to the Scriptures and this error needs to be publicly aired lest the naïve and slow-witted be further deluded (there is no excuse for others who have heard the Gospel and rejected it). The evolutionists need to be ashamed of their claim of evolving from a monkey limb of the man-made evolutionary tree. If an evolutionist has the audacity to bold-facedly confess his kinship to the monkey family, nothing else should taint his reputation or should embarrass him.

The Greatest Hoax

Evolution is the second greatest hoax perpetrated upon mankind! What is the greatest hoax perpetrated upon mankind since the creation of the world? The writer believes that two of the greatest lies of all time is: 1) the false religious dogma of obtaining salvation by good works and, 2) the authority of church ordinances (baptism; communion; holy water; et al) to save a soul (refer to the writer's booklet, *Can Water Baptism Save?*).

Of course, religionists will mix works with grace in spite of the plain teachings of Scriptures (Ephesians 2:8, 9; Romans 4:4-6; 11:6). Scriptures expressly forbid mixing grace and works together. Salvation by "works" demands the same kind of heathen faith that pagans and wicked Israelites possessed when they sacrificed their children to dung-hill deities (2 Chronicles 33:6; Ezekiel 16:21).

83

Salvation is solely by God's grace (free) through faith and without works (Ephesians 2:8-10; Titus 3:5; Romans 3:20, 28; 6:23; Galatians 2:16, 21). Leaders of false religions mislead people into believing that faith coupled with ordinances and good works impute salvation. Salvation is **all of grace without works** and rituals (Romans 11:6; 4:3-6).

Salvation is a gift (free) from God upon the sinner's genuine repentance (not the invented *penance* of religion) and belief upon Christ as his Lord and Saviour (Luke 13:3; Ephesians 2:8-9: Romans 6:23; Galatians 2:16; Romans 3:20; 4:4-6; 10:9-10, 13). Again, religionists erroneously attribute works and sacraments (mixed with faith) for salvation instead of repentance and faith. Of course, salvation is a "gift." Gift means free of works.

How does science fit into the picture of resurrection and life?

Even believers of true science (as opposed to bogus science) cannot comprehend the supernatural workings of God. True believers accept Biblical statements by faith, not proof. The Holy Spirit bears witness with our spirit (Romans 8:16).

Scientists can simulate the physical composition of a seed with the exact known amounts of chemical elements (carbon, nitrogen, hydrogen, oxygen, phosphorus, sulfur, manganese, potassium, sodium, selenium, etc., yet they cannot initiate a spark of life into it (cause the seed to germinate). Of course, some elements are present in trace amounts of PPM - parts per million,

The writer is aware that secular scientists of *evolution infamy* make claims of producing live cells in their laboratory experiments. Their claims of producing life in the test tube (in vitro fertilization) are totally fallacious (The cloned sheep, Dolly, is an example). They are only manipulating live cells that already exist. Man cannot create anything. Man cannot even create inanimate matter (lifeless substance) much less matter containing life. The First Law of Thermodynamics, *The Law of Conservation of Matter* says, "Matter cannot be created nor destroyed, but only changed in form." Life only comes from life that already exists and is given of God. Only the Creator could create new matter, as He did when He multiplied the loaves and fishes, or new energy, as He did when He walked on the water and when He stilled the storm waves with a Word. The world and all things within were made by God and sustained by Him (John 1:3, 10; Colossians 1:16).

Chemistry does not support evolution's vain jangling

Evolutionists suppose that a random accumulation of chemicals (Viz., a primordial soup of carbon, hydrogen, nitrogen, oxygen, phosphorus, sulfur, et al) simmered for millions of years and formed a single cell of life that eventually formed a multi-cellular something and eventually became a monkey, then a college professor, and finally a man. (The college professor is lower on the evolutionary scale than man!) However, life only comes from life, not chemicals. To be sure, chemicals are necessary to sustain life, but they sure do not generate or produce life. This supposition of chemicals producing life leads us back to the old heathen evolutionary philosophy of 'Spontaneous Generation'.

(<u>Spontaneous generation</u>: the theory, now discredited, that living organisms can originate in nonliving matter independently of other living matter; abiogenesis --*Webster's New World College Dictionary*, Fourth Edition.)

About 'spontaneous generation' (abiogenesis), there was a time when gullible evolutionists actually believed in it. Just leave meat outside to rot, and miraculously maggots appear, seemingly from nowhere! Did the maggots spontaneously generate from rotting meat? (Of course, insects such as flies lay eggs that hatch and feed on rotting substances.) Evolutionists today, out of one side of their mouths, deny the possibility of spontaneous generation, but dogmatically affirm it from the other side of their mouth (under the guise of calling it naturalism). As previously stated, life cannot come from non-life. Life reproduces (generates; propagates; brings forth others of its kind) from its own seed. The Lord Jesus Christ created every living system and sustains them even today (Colossians 1:16, 17).

Chemicals or dead matter do not contain an iota of the promise and potential of life. **A.C. Dixon** says:

> -In dead **vegetation** matter, there is the promise and potency of decomposition.

> -In dead **animal** matter, there is the promise and potency of putrefaction.

-in dead **minerals**, there is the promise and potency of more death. (emphasis by the writer)

Dixon says that embryonic, immature life has no power to reproduce itself. Eggs never hatch eggs; apples never bear apples—it takes a hen to hatch an egg. Babies never bear babies. Immature, embryonic life is absolutely un-reproductive. It cannot multiply itself. It is un-improvable. You cannot improve embryonic life by working on it. How do you improve the quality of eggs? By making a better quality of hen. If you try to improve any kind of embryonic life, you endanger its existence. You have to work on the mature product.

Pseudo-science (of the past)

Science Once Said	Now Science Changed its Position
There were only 1,100 stars	There are innumerable stars
Light was fixed in place	Light does indeed move
Air was weightless	Yes, air has weight
The wind blew straight	Winds blow in different directions and in circular directions
The earth was flat	The earth is a sphere
Sick people needed to be bled	Blood is the source of life

<u>The Bible had it right from the start</u>...

1. There are innumerable stars (Jeremiah 33:22).

2. Light does indeed move (Job 38:19, 20).

3. Yes, air has weight ((Job 28:25).

4. Winds blow in different direction and in circular motion (Ecclesiastes 1:6).

5. The earth is a sphere (Isaiah 40:22).

6. Blood is the source of life (Leviticus 17:11).

Secular evolutionary science was wrong even before technology could prove otherwise. The Bible has stood the test of time. It should be noted that *mature* Christians have never believed in the evolutionary pseudo-science of the past nor do they believe the idiotic, vain babblings of the present day evolutionists. This writer would be too ashamed to claim a monkey as an uncle ("But if any man be ignorant, let him be ignorant" – I Corinthians 14:38). Getting down to plain truth, you either believe God's Word or the ever-vacillating grunts of ape-men (evolutionists).

John 8:32: And ye shall know the truth,
and the truth shall make you free.

Debates between evolutionists and creationists

At the time of the initial publishing of this paper (2006), one religious source reported that there were over 300 debates between creation scientists and evolution scientists. According to their audiences, practically all of the debates were won by creationists. Why? It was not because the creationists were intellectually smarter but because the real facts of science support Creation!

Creationists often endure personal insults and debate trickery. There was one occasion when a creationist lost a debate! For practice, a creationist assumed the role of an atheist and was defeated by another fellow creationist. Those who accept the Bible are wiser if not smarter.

If any evolutionist reading this booklet desires to publicly debate the issue, the writer will gladly make an effort to furnish a creationist opponent.

Over time, this writer has grown weary of evolutionary terminologies such as: "4.6 billion years ago," "lush habitat," "succulent plants" and evolutionary mechanisms of "may have, might have, could have, or probably." How foolish to hinge one's everlasting soul upon such vain "may haves" and empty philosophies!

The spiritually bankrupt evolutionist faults the creationist for accepting the Genesis account of creation. The writer pities the evolutionist for his blind devotion to evolution. *Genesis chapter 1* tells us that God created it all. The writer believes the Bible unequivocally. Anyone that does not believe the Bible is himself standing upon a slippery slope in a dark place at a very late hour. His pride will be his doom.

> *Romans 13:12: The night is far spent, the day is at hand: let us therefore cast off the works of darkness, and let us put on the armour of light.*

True science is both *miraculous* and *natural* and will always agree with the Bible

Science does not judge the Bible's accuracy. Although the Bible is not, technically speaking a science book, it does judge the accuracy of science.

Men have tried for centuries to find errors in Scriptures and have *alleged* all sorts of contradictions in God's Word. The Bible has withstood the onslaught of the anemic skeptics for centuries. **The Word of God** shall stand forever (Isaiah 40:8; Matthew 24:35; I Peter 1:25).

Evolution is nothing more than "false science." As previously mentioned, the Gnostics boasted of their "false science" (false knowledge) in the NT book of Timothy.

> *I Timothy 6:20: O Timothy, keep that which is committed to thy trust, avoiding profane and vain babblings, and oppositions of* **science falsely so called**.

(Science: Gk. "Gnosis" or knowledge)

An atheist once said, "The bigger the **lie**, the easier it is to believe." Another atheist said, "Tell a **lie** often enough and some will believe it."

Evolution is the "Big One." Evolution is one of the most preposterous deceptions perpetrated upon mankind since the serpent beguiled Eve in the Garden of Eden.

Hostility of atheists and evolutionists toward Biblical Creation

Atheists and evolutionists censure any thought that doesn't support evolution. Why? They are supporting their own private agenda. They are letting their insecurities hang out. Evolutionists cannot support their incredible hypothesis with facts. They are admitting that evolution cannot stand the test of true science. Why should the evolutionist get so disturbed at the mention of Biblical creation as a world-view if he has all of the facts? Actually, the anger of the evolutionist against the Creation account of Scriptures is quite simple; he rejects the authority of God's Word. Many of them are rebels, haters of God, and bloated with pride. Evolutionists are in rebellion against their Creator and most are so naïve as to be totally unaware of the satanic influence in their lives.

(**NOTE**: the writer is aware that evolutionists and atheists do not believe in a real Satan and devils, but the day is coming that they will - Philippians 2:10-11; Revelation 20:12.

There are no atheists and evolutionists in Hell now and neither will there ever be.)

Stem-cell research does not support the claims of evolution

Stem cell research in the early embryonic stage of life is just another form of abortion. The writer is in accord with Dr. John D. Morris' sentiments concerning Stem Cell Research.

91

Dr. Morris says,

"Since it involves the "harvesting" of living human tissue, everyone recognizes the difficult ethical questions involved...Human stem cells are those embryonic cells which result from the uniting of human egg and sperm and the first few cell divisions to follow. These magnificent cells carry the potential to construct any type of cell-flesh, blood, bone, teeth, heart, liver, hair, etc...By harvesting the original stem cells before their specialization and by controlling their environment and later growth, medical science hopes to be able to regenerate damaged tissue in patients."

Biologists know that life comes from life—that there is not time during which life ceases and then restarts—thus, the inescapable conclusion that the new life begins at conception. In humans, life does not begin after the first trimester, or when the fetus could survive outside the womb. The only defensible, logical position is that it begins at conception. The cessation of that life must be called death, and its willful death constitutes murder.

Creationists additionally recognize human life as "the image of God," to be valued and protected...

Thus the question, 'Should the stem cells of an unborn human be harvested to save the life of an ill human?... Should one life be valued over another?'...

Much of this destructive impulse derives from possible huge profits as well as personal pride" (*Institute For Creation Research* ©2001, *Back to Genesis*, November 2001, P.O. Box 2667, El Cajon, CA 92021).

Stem cell ("embryonic") research supports the horrendous slaughter of the innocent unborn. The unborn aborted baby would have grown into an adult if not butchered by the heathen doctor. Having a doctoral degree in medicine does not remove the pagan character of man. A doctoral degree may only have the effect of producing an educated pagan. Someone has said, "The Ph.D. attached to the end of a man's name is no more than a curl in a pig's tail that doesn't help the ham at all."

Richard Sumner (*The Biblical Evangelist*) says,

> "There is strong evidence adult stem cells may work as well (as embryonic). In laboratory tests involving animals, "adult stem cells were able to produce the ball structure of a joint." Embryonic stem cells are taken from aborted babies, which require murdering the unborn child to provide medical cures for the sick. Healthy adult stem cells can be harvested without destroying the donor. For the Christian, only the adult stem cells are ethical *(The Biblical Evangelist,* January-February, *2004,* p. 14, *Significant Trends).*

The secular university professor's denial of Biblical truth

Many *all-knowing* secular professors (of course, not all) mock at the mere mention of Biblical Creation and even the existence of Hell as a literal place; however, they readily accept the un-provable hypothesis of evolution beginnings ("...broad is the way" - Matthew 7:13). The poor muddle-headed, secular, university professor is sure that eternal retribution (Hell) is just a mythological aberration (disorder) in the minds of incurably religious folk. These unbelieving secularists are too dense to consider the power of God in changing the lives of liars, thieves, adulterers, fornicators, sodomites, and murderers. "And such **were** some of you..." (I Corinthians 6:11). Notice the past-tense verb, "were."

Proponents of evolution merely emulate their mentor's teachings ("monkey see, monkey do"). Again, after all related issues are explored and thoroughly debated, it all boils down to 'willing ignorance' and rebellion against God's Word.

> Psalms 14:1: "The fool hath said in his heart, There is no God..."

Missing links taught in the public school textbooks

Missing links are still missing. They only exist in the hearts and minds of naïve evolutionists, ignoramuses, and unbelievers (Proverbs 6:18; Romans 1:21; 2 Corinthians 10:4-5).

Most of the evolutionist's missing links have **long ago** been debunked as fraud and fake (Big Daddy tract booklet, Chick Publications, pp. 11, 12 and The Collapse of Evolution, pp. 134-138, Baker Books, Grand Rapids, Michigan 49516)

For example:

- **Heidelberg Man:** Built from a jaw bone that was conceded by many to be quite human.

- **Nebraska Man:** Scientifically built up from one tooth, later found to be the tooth of an extinct pig. At the famous Scopes evolution trial in Dayton, Tennessee, the Nebraska Man evidence was presented by the leading scientific authorities of that day as proof of evolution. They scoffed and laughed at William Jennings Bryan, when he protested the scanty evidence. This "tooth" evidence was supposed to have come from a prehistoric man who supposedly lived one million years age. However, years later, when more fossils were unearthed, it was discovered that Nebraska Man was only a pig (a pig make a monkey out of an evolutionist!) – *Have You Been Brainwashed*", Duane T. Gish, Ph.D.

- **Piltdown Man:** The jawbone turned out to belong to a modern ape. This hoax was published by a *Readers Digest,* dated October 1956. The jawbone actually belonged to an ape that died only fifty years previously. The teeth were filed down, and both teeth and bones were discolored with bichromate of potash to conceal their true identity. The "experts" were easily fooled.

- **Peking Man:** Supposedly 500,000 years old, but all evidence has disappeared.

- **Neanderthal Man:** At the Int'l. Congress of Zoology (1958), Dr. A.J.E. Cave said his examination showed that this famous skeleton found in France over 50 years ago is that of an old man who suffered from arthritis. Some think that his bowed legs were caused by the lack of Vitamin D (his habitat in lush forests did not allow sufficient sunshine). Today,

Neanderthal Man is classified as Homo sapiens, completely human.

- **New Guinea Man:** Dates away back to 1970. This species has been found in the region just north of Australia (alive and well).

- **Cro-Magnon Man:** One of the earliest and best established fossils is at least equal in physique and brain capacity to modern man...so what's the difference?

- **Modern Man:** This genius thinks we came from a monkey

    Romans 1:22: "...professing themselves to be wise they became fools."

Do not anticipate any forth-coming expose from your government-regulated schools concerning these concocted evolutionary-links. However, you may expect the oxymoron, "Deafening Silence."

John D. Morris says,

"If you don't know what a missing link is, don't worry. No one knows what a missing link is, because they are missing! Evolution depends on *innumerable* missing links (*intermediate steps*), each of which lived in the unobserved past and have gone extinct, replaced by their evermore evolved descendants. While we don't really know what a missing link is (or was), we can know what they should be. As each type evolves into something else, there should be numerous in-between types, each stage gaining more and more traits of the descendant while losing traits of the ancestor. The missing links which should be present in abundance, are still missing. Evolution says links existed whether or not we find them. The fact is we don't find them."

Sir John Ambrose Fleming said,

"Evolution is essentially atheistic and is actually an attempt to dispense with the very idea of God and substitute for an Intelligent Creator an impersonal non-intelligent agency, namely mutations, time, chance, and natural selection." As a professor at a major university, Fleming carefully researched the evidence for Darwinism, concluding that the theory is not supported by science (*Acts and Facts*, November 2009, p. 14).

It is an easily observable fact that error, atheism, and idolatry have a strong attraction for those who refuse to worship the true God of the Bible.

Dr. Duane T. Gish says,

"Darwinists assume that life, or the primitive cell, arose by pure chance. By chance, nothingness developed into substance. That evolved into a very highly complex organization...without a designer...all life gradually evolved from a single cell, which had evolved from dead matter. (Where did the matter come from?) For example by chance some amino acids were formed. Then from these the necessary protein was formed. The probability of a protein of only 50 amino acids forming by chance would be-1/10 with the exponential number 65, or in layman language... ...100,000,000,000,000,000,000,0 00,000,000,000,000,000,000,000,000,000,

000,000,000 to One" (*Have You Been Brainwashed*, Dr. Duane T. Gish, published by Life Messenger, Box 1967, Seattle, WA. 98111).

One 'mathematical probability expert' says that an exponential number of 50 zeros or more makes the probability of happening impossible.

The writer cannot think of but two things that would support the evolutionist's dream of beginnings: 1) the fossil record; 2) man's vain philosophical worldviews.

It is quite obvious that the fossil record does not support evolution. That only leaves the speculations, opinions, and wild fantasies and dreams of secular humanists.

If "origins" of evolution were supported by facts, the transitional forms (changes between one kind of animal to another kind) in the fossil record would be innumerable (quadrillions) compared to the basic kinds themselves. The *missing links* cannot be found and will never be found...except in the dreams and imaginations of bankrupt evolutionists.

Charles Darwin admitted that,

"As by this theory innumerable forms must have existed, why do we not find them embedded in countless numbers in the crust of the earth? The number of intermediate links, between all living and extinct species, must have been inconceivably great."

The late **Professor R. Goldschmidt** of the University of California observed,

> "It is good to keep in mind...that nobody has ever succeeded in producing even one new species by the accumulation of micromutations."

Ray Simmons says,

> "There is a standing offer of $250,000 for anyone who can present scientifically verifiable evidence to demonstrate a single instance in which one "kind" has ever evolved into another "kind." No one has come forward to claim the quarter-million dollars" *(The Times Examiner,* September 8, 1999, P.4, Column, *"From a Christian Perspective").*

If the writer remembers correctly, **Dr. John R. Rice (**former editor of *The Sword of the Lord* newspaper), for many years before his death, offered $10,000 dollars for proof of any factual errors in the Bible. As any reader knows, the Bible teaches creation, not theistic evolution or devil-lution. Any proof of evolution would disprove the Bible. As far as this writer knows, no one ever attempted to claim the money. As Martin Luther said long ago, "When the Scripture speak, God speaks" (sola scriptura).

Jesus' evaluation of Scripture, **"Have you not read...?"** (cf.. Luke 6:3; Mark 2:25; 12:10; Matthew 12:3; 19:4).

> *Isaiah 40:8: The grass withereth, the flower fadeth: but the Word of our God shall stand for ever.*

99

John Grebe, director of basic and nuclear research for Dow Chemical Company, is offering $1,000 to anyone who can produce just one clear proof of evolution (*The Collapse of Evolution*, p. 158).

(**Note:** Grebe is not a fly-by-night John Doe; he has over 100 patents and is responsible for the development of Styrofoam, synthetic rubber, and Saran Wrap.)

Many secular scientists are turning away from evolution and turning to Creation. Washington scholar **Dean Overman** declares, "Beyond reasonable doubt, there has to be a Creator," citing new discoveries in microbiology and the exquisitely precise laws of physics. Overman *is a* 54-year-old member of MENSA, an international society of geniuses. Overman says**:**

> • ...the odds that life evolved by random chance are smaller than the odds of hitting a housefly on a wall on the other side of the universe with a single unaimed rifle shot;
>
> • ...or smaller than the odds of a monkey with a typewriter in a few billion years randomly typing out the sonnets of Shakespeare.

Many modern-day scientists insist that,

> "math and physics can prove what the theologians ask us to take on faith, that the universe that spawned life could not be a product of mere chance." Many such books now offer "proof" of what they call "Intelligent Design" (Hugh Pyle's "News and Views," *Sword of the Lord*, page 6, April 17, 1998)

Duane T. Gish says,

"Even Sir Fred Hoyle, an atheist and evolutionist, one of the world's foremost astronomers, has abandoned that theory and now calls himself a creationist--even though, as far as we know, he makes no pretense of being a Christian" (*The Biblical Evangelist*, May-June, 1999, p. 2).

In November 1999, **National Geographic Magazine** featured a "missing link" dinosaur-bird called *Archaeoraptor*. The birdlike upper torso and the tail and feet of a small raptor, was described by the magazine as a "true missing link in the complex chain that connects dinosaurs and birds." Archaeoraptor (unofficial name) is actually two animals pieced together either as an honest mistake made by its discoverers in China or as a breathtaking forgery. **Storrs Olson**, curator of birds at the Smithsonian Institution's Natural History Museum and an outspoken skeptic of the bird-dinosaur link, says he warned the magazine in November, when the article was published, that there were serious problems with the fossil. He says he was ignored. USA TODAY, 1/25/00. (*Sword of the Lord*, 3/17/2000, Noteworthy News Notes, page 8)

You can be sure that the truth of the discovery will quietly fizzle out with little fanfare!

The evolutionists relentlessly search for a transitional bridge from ape to man. Another of their darling candidates of late is Ardi (*Ardipithecus ramidus*), a four-foot female constructed of fragments of shattered bones. She (or it) was found about 1994 along the Awash River in Ethopia. In his assessment of the significance of *Ardipithecus ramidus*, bipedality expert C. Owen Lovejoy wrote, "We can no longer rely on homologies with African apes for accounts of our origins and must turn instead to general evolutionary theory" (Lovejoy, C. O. 2009, *Reexamining Human Origin in Light of Ardipithecus ramidus,* Science. 326 (5949): 74el. Brian Thomas said, "Thus, setting aside evolution inspired ideology, there is no scientific reason---or observed evidence---to believe that Ardi was an ancestor of mankind. In fact, there is every reason to believe it is solely an extinct primate, as uniquely created as any monkey still alive today (*Acts and Facts,* November 2009, pp. 8, 9).

Very few uneducated people have been exposed to the *vain janglings* (I Timothy 1:6) of evolutionary academia; consequently, many people of the "un-indoctrinated" and "un-brainwashed" segment of American society still hold to Bible Creation.

High school science teachers and secular university professors who teach evolution of origins are willingly ignorant (2 Peter 3:5). They are part of the problem; the Bible is the sure answer.

{**vain janglings:** empty and useless talk}

The writer is not down-grading true education and is thankful for his very small measure of college training. Of course, there are many intelligent and educated people as well as uneducated intelligent people that believe in Biblical Creation. All people of academia are not *willingly ignorant* and *dumbed-down* by contemporary *educrats.* (**educrats:** bungling inept educators)

102

Uneducated pipe-smoking grandmothers have far too much common sense to swallow evolution's incredible line of hypothetical malarkey.

Future shock awaits many unbelievers

In the writer's college Sociology class, a film named *Future Shock* was viewed as part of the sociology course. This film was titled *Future Shock* because it depicted bold and shocking future human behavior and trends. This aberrant behavior was considered a *cultural shock*. The writer believes that this cultural shock does not even compare to the horrible shock that awaits unbelievers and scoffers when they close their eyes in death and opens them in Hell fire (Gehenna). The atheists and evolutionists had better enjoy their laughs now for they will never, never laugh again after death. As previously stated, there will be no atheists in Hell. -See Mark 9:42-48; Luke 16:19-31.

Romans 1:22: Professing themselves to be wise, they became fools.

Mathematical logistics of fulfilled Biblical prophecies prove that Jesus is the Creator

Jesus created the world and He sustains it (Colossians 1:16-17). The odds in favor of Creation and against evolution is overwhelming. Prophetical fulfillments clearly resolve any question of the deity of Jesus and His Creation.

William W. Orr said in his booklet, *Can we Be Sure Jesus Christ Is God,*

> "If you were to measure the chance that over 300 differing prophecies would happen to converge on one man, the law of probability would demand a sum calling for more zeros that there are letters in all the words of an unabridged dictionary!"

Many Bible scholars say that there are 333 Old Testament prophecies related to Christ's first coming.

(**Note:** The writer is not a mathematician nor a probability statistician and the following probabilities may contain a margin of error; however lesser numbers would still speak great volumes.)

Astronomical numbers supporting the fulfillment of specific prophecies:

- The probability that one man could fulfill one prophecy in 300 is *"one in 300."*

- The probability that one man could fulfill two prophecies in 300 is *"one in 90,000."*

- The probability that one man could fulfill three prophecies in 300 is *"one in 27 million"* ("one in 27,000,000").

- The probability that one man could fulfill four prophecies in 300 is *"one in 8 billion and 100 million"* ("one in 8,100,000,000").

- The probability that one man could fulfill five prophecies in 300 is *"one in 2 trillion and 430 billion"* ("one in 2,430,000,000,000").

- The probability that one man could fulfill six prophecies in 300 is *"one in*

729 trillion" ("one in 729,000,000,000,000").

• The probability that one man could fulfill seven prophecies in 300 is *"one in*

218 quadrillion and 700 trillion" ("one in 218,700,000,000,000,000").

• The probability that one man could fulfill eight prophecies in 300 is *"one in 65 quintillion and 610 quadrillion"* ("one in $65,610^{15}$").

• The probability that one man could fulfill nine prophecies in 300 is *"one in 19 sextillion and 683 quintillion"* ("one in $19,683,^{18}$").

• The probability that one man could fulfill ten prophecies in 300 is *"one in 5 septillion, 904 sextillion and 900 quintillion"* ("one in $5,904,900^{24}$").

The writer has not attempted to locate all 333 prophecies relating to the First Coming of Christ but is aware of about 100 of them. Even if there were only 100 prophecies fulfilled, the chances that only 10 out of the 100 being fulfilled would be "one in one-hundred quintillion" (one in 100^{30}).

Dave Hunt says,

> "The Old Testament contains more than 300 prophetic references to the coming Messiah that were fulfilled in the life, death, and the resurrection of Jesus. Sixty of these are considered to be major prophecies. If we eliminate 12 of these as within the power of Jesus and for His disciples to deliberately fulfill, that leaves 48. Professor Peter Stoner calculated the odds to be 10 to the 157th

power that 48 such prophecies could be fulfilled by chance in Jesus Christ. In probability theory, it is generally agreed that any odds smaller than 10 to the fiftieth power are the same as zero. Since 10 to the 157th power is 10 to the 107th power (that's a 1 with 107 zeros after it) smaller than 10 to the 50th power, we can safely say that the fulfillment by Jesus of these 48 specific prophecies proved conclusively that He is the Messiah" *(Peace, Prosperity, & The Coming Holocaust, p. 100).*

As one writer stated,

"an incomprehensible mathematical monstrosity."

Only the God-man Jesus Christ, the Creator of all things, could accomplish this.

Messianic prophecies fulfilled by Jesus

• His birth (Genesis 3:15; 49:10; Daniel 9:26; Luke 2:11-20)

• Place of His birth in Bethlehem (Micah 5:2; Matthew 2:6; John 7:42)

• Be born of a virgin (Isaiah 7:14; Jeremiah 31.22; Matthew 1:23)

• Be born the seed of a woman (Genesis 3:15; Matthew 1:18-23; Luke 1:27-35; 2:33)

• Be born the seed of Abraham (Genesis 22:18; Matthew 1:1-16)

• Born of the lineage of the tribe of Judah (Genesis 49:8-10; Matthew 1; 3, 16; Luke 3:23, 33; Revelation 5:5)

- Be called out of Egypt (Hosea 11:1; Matthew 2:15)

- Heir to the throne of David (Isaiah 9:6, 7; Matthew 1:1)

- Time of His first coming (Daniel 9:25; Galatians 4:4)

- Prominent persons would visit Him at His birth (Genesis 60:3)

- Praised by little children (Psalms 8:2; Matthew 21:4-5)

- Innocent children would be slaughtered because of a vile, jealous king (Jeremiah 31:15; Matthew 2:17)

- Proclaim a jubilee to the world (Isaiah 58:6; 61:1; Luke 4:18, 19)

- Dwell in Nazareth (Isaiah 11:1; Matthew 2:23)

- The coming Saviour would be a prophet like Moses (Deuteronomy 18:15; Matthew 17:3; John 1:17; 3:14; 5:46, 47)

- Be a priest after Melchizedek (Psalms 110:4; Hebrews 5:6; 6:20; 7:21)

- Ministry in Galilee (Isaiah 9:2; Matthew 4:15)

- His ministry one of healing (Isaiah 53:4; Matthew 8:17)

- Declared to be the Son of God (Psalms 2:7; Matthew 16:16; 27:43, 54)

- His ministry would be characterized by miracles (Isaiah 61:1; Luke 4:18, 19)

- His miracles would not be believed (Isaiah 53:1; John 12:37-38)

- He would be zealous for the Father (Psalms 69:9; 119:139; John 6:37-40)

- Heralded by John the Baptist (Isaiah 40:3; Malachi 3:1; Matthew 11:10; Luke 7:27; Mark 1:2)

- Anointed with the Spirit (Isaiah 61:1; Luke 4:18, 19)

- Anointed to preach (Isaiah 61:1; Luke 4:18, 19)

- Filled with God's Spirit (Psalms 45:7; Isaiah 11:2; 61:1-2; Luke 4:18-19)

- Adored by great men (Psalms 72:10; Matthew 2:1-11; 27:57, 58; John 3:1, 2)

- Rides into Jerusalem upon a colt the foal of an ass (Isaiah 62:11; Psalms 118:26; Zechariah 9:9; Matthew 21:1-11)

- He would heal many (Isaiah 53:4; Matthew 8:16-17)

- He would speak in parables (Psalms 78:2; Isaiah 6:9-10; Matthew 13:10-15)

- Rejected by His brethren (Psalms 69:8; John 7:3-5)

- That He would be the rejected cornerstone (Isaiah 53:1; John 12:37-38)

- Rejected by the rulers (Isaiah 6:10; 29:13; 53:1; Psalms 69:4; Matthew 15:8, 9; 21:42; Luke 20:17)

- Hated without a cause (Psalms 35:19; John 15:25)

- Accused by false witnesses (Zechariah 13:7; Acts 1:9)

- Betrayed by a friend (Psalms 41:9; Matthew 26:31, 67; Mark 14:27, 65; 15:19; John 13:18, 19)

- Rejected (Isaiah 53:3)

- Be sold for 30 pieces of silver (Zechariah 11:12; Matthew 26:15; 27:9, 10)

- Betrayal price used to buy a "Potter's Field" (Zechariah 11:13; Matthew 27:7)

- Forsaken by His disciples (Zechariah 13:7; Matthew 26:31, 56)

- He would be a man of sorrows (Isaiah 53:3; Matthew 26:37-38)

- Be dumb before His accusers (Isaiah 53:7; Matthew 26:62; Mark 15:3-5; Luke 23:9; John 19:9; Acts 8:32, 33)

- Be scourged, His face spit on, His hair plucked, His cheeks smitten (Isaiah 50:5, 6; Matthew 26:67; 27:30; Mark 14:65; 15:19)

- His garments parted and lots cast (Psalms 22:18; Matthew 27:35; Luke 23:34)

- Surrounded and mocked by His enemies (Psalms 22:7-8; Matthew 27:39-44; Mark15:29-32)

- People sit and stare (Psalms 22:17; Matthew 27:36)

- He would be crucified between two thieves (Isaiah 53:12; Matthew 27:38; Mark 15:27)

- They shoot out the lip, they shake the head (Psalms 22:7; 109:25; Matthew 27:39)

- Hands and feet pierced (Psalms 22:16; Zechariah 12:10; 13:6; John 19:34; 20:25-27)

- His friends would stand afar off (Psalms 38:11; 88:8; Isaiah 63:3; Luke 23:49)

- Agonize with thirst (Psalms 22:15; 69:3, 21; Matthew 27:34, 48; John 19:28)

- Be given gall and vinegar to drink (Psalms 69:21; Matthew 27:34; John 19:29)

- Not a bone of His body broken (Psalms 34:20; Exodus 12:46; Numbers 9:12; John 19:36)

- Made intercession for transgressors and murderers (Isaiah 53:12; Luke 23:32)

- Dying words foretold (Psalms 22:1; 31:5; Matthew 27:46; Mark 15:34; Luke 23:46)

- Willingly gave up His life (Isaiah 50:6; 53:12; Daniel 9:26; Matthew 20:28; John 10:11, 18; Galatians 2:20; I Corinthians 15:3; Hebrews 1:3; I Peter 2:24; Revelation 1:5)

- Forsaken by God (Psalms 22:1; Matthew 27:46)

- Cut off (Daniel 9:26; John 3:16; I Corinthians 15:3,4; I Timothy 3:16)

- Crucified Christ hidden by darkness (Amos 8:9; Psalms 22:2; Matthew 27:45)

- His heel bruised (Genesis 3:15; Matthew 27:34, 35; Luke 23:33)

- Die with malefactors (Isaiah 53:12; Matthew 27:44; Luke 23:33, 39-43)

- Pierced (Zechariah 12:10; Psalms 22:16)

- Buried in a rich man's tomb (Isaiah 53:9; Matthew 27:57-60)

- His body would not disintegrate (Psalms 16:10; Acts 2:27)

- His resurrection foretold (Isaiah 26:19; Psalms 16:10-11; Luke 24:17)

- His ascension foretold (Psalms 68:18; 110:1; Mark 16:9, 14-19)

- He would become a greater high priest than Aaron (Psalms 110:4; Hebrews 5:4-6, 10; 7:11-28)

- He would be seated at God's right hand (Psalms 110:1; Matthew 22:44; Hebrews 10:12-13)

- Conversion of Gentiles unto Him (Isaiah 11:10; Romans 15:12)

- His rejection would be followed by the destruction of Jerusalem and great tribulation (Daniel 9:27; 11:31; 12:1, 11; Matthew 24:15; Mark 13:14; Luke 21:20)

- The Word of God shall stand forever (Isaiah 40:8; Psalms 12:6, 7; Matthew 24:35; Luke 21:33)

There are many more fulfilled prophecies that could be listed here, but for the sake of time and space, the writer will stop here.

The mathematical probabilities or proofs of evolution

Answer: zilch; zero; nada; none. It is mathematically impossible to prove evolution! In short, evolution is no more than psycho-babble of a disengaged brainstem.

Sir Fred Hoyle, world-famous British astronomer, declared after researching the probability of an evolutionary origin of life,

> "The probability of a naturalistic evolutionary origin of life anywhere in the universe in 20 billion years is equal to the probability that a tornado sweeping through a junkyard would assemble a Boeing 747."

Sir Fred, **formerly an atheist**, declared life therefore had to be created, therefore there must be a God. The all-pervasive existence of design and purpose seen throughout the universe and in every detail of the structure and function of living organisms speak eloquently of the existence of the Designer - (Copyright 2004 by ICR, *Impact #375*, September 2004, by Duane T. Gish)

A noted Jewish archaeologist stated,

> "It may be stated categorically that no archaeological discovery has ever controverted {contradicted; denied} a biblical reference." (*Acts & Facts*, Institute for Creation Research, p. 5, Origins Issues, www.icr.org).

Even the anti-God devils have enough sense to acknowledge the existence of God:

> *James 2:19: Thou believest that there is one God; thou doest well: the devils also believe, and tremble.*

The moral aspects of evolution

If evolution is true, there are no moral aspects for humanity; there is no objective standard to measure what is right and what is wrong. If

112

evolution is true, neither the creationists nor the evolutionists are correct in moral judgments. One person killing another is the same as a lion killing a deer or a cat killing a mouse. Mores (beneficial societal moral conduct) simply become formal legal code or societal laws void of God.

If evolution is true, forget about teaching children against fornication, gambling, lying, stealing, and even bad manners. Some might even justify Hitler's murderous rule (making a super-race) under evolution standards.

If evolutionists do lead moral lives, they have no grounds upon which to judge the behavior of others as wrong or even a reason for leading a moral life themselves. When we instruct children against lying, murder, and hate, it is because our Creator God has told us it is wrong, in His Word, the Bible.

If evolution is true, shut down all of the churches, call home all of the missionaries, teach no honorable truths, lie and cheat to get ahead, insult your parents when it suits you, and kill for your advantage; after all, when your die, you are just as a dead dog...according to evolutionists.

If evolution is true and there is no resurrection and we die as a dog, "...let us eat and drink; for tomorrow we die" (I Corinthians 15:32). Evolutionists have a baseless moral standard.

If evolution is true, by deduction the Bible would be false because it teaches Creation which is totally opposed to evolution. There is no third choice!

If evolution is absolute truth, produce all of the innumerable, tangible proofs. Of course, there is not even ONE single proof.

As previously reported, atheist and vehement anti-creationist **Dr. Eugenie Scott**, in a magazine interview, once stated:

> "I have found that the most effective allies for evolution are people of the faith community. One clergyman with a backward collar is worth two biologists at a school board meeting any day!" (*The Voice in the Wilderness*, p. 14, June 2005)

Someone has well said,

> "Man-made religion has no value except as fodder for spiritually impoverished evolutionists".

Evolutionists are afraid

Evolutionists reject Biblical Creation as a possibility because they reject the *supernatural* working of the God of the Bible. They insist upon *natural* explanations for all phenomena. Our God is a miracle working God. Divine revelation will not convince the evolutionists either, in spite of overwhelming evidence that **the Bible is the written Word of God**. The majority of the people in the USA (and possibly the world) believe in Creation. Legislation for the inclusion of the scientific evidence for creation along with evolution has been proposed but is opposed by evolutionary legislation. Evolutionists use the phony smokescreen of church/state separation. It has been shown that the First Amendment was never intended to remove God or Creation from the schools. Most of the support for public schools comes from taxpayers who don't believe in evolution. Do our opinions count for anything? If the leaders of evolution are so supremely confident that science proves evolution (so they say), **why are they afraid** to confront a hint of Creation or theology into the public schools? **The evolutionists are hypocritical** in that they have always argued in favor of academic freedom but have refused to admit any others the same privilege. Of course, they only intend academic freedom for themselves.

Bible authority is the only reliable authority for origins

- **Theologian James Orr** stated,

  "No stronger proof could be afforded of the truth and sublimity of the biblical account of the origin of things than is given by the comparison of the narrative of creation in Genesis 1:1-2:4, with the mythological cosmogonies and theogonies found in other religions" (Glueck, N. *Rivers in the Desert*, Philadelphia: Jewish Publ. Society, 1969, p.84).

- **Josh McDowell** stated,

  "There is more evidence for the historical reliability of the New Testament than any ten pieces of classical literature considered" (*Acts & Facts*, Institute for Creation Research, p. 5, Origins Issues, www.icr.org). Of course, the New Testament teaches "creation."

There is hope for the unbeliever to change while he lives (none after death). Anyone with enough faith to accept the ludicrous hypothesis of evolution (which does not have a stitch of credibility) certainly has enough faith to believe that God created it all and sustains it all (Colossians 1:16, 17).

Actually, some former atheists and agnostics have now converted to Christianity and are some of the more accomplished scientists and stronger contenders for Biblical Creation. They were wise enough to think for themselves and seek out truth (John 8:32) even as did Lew Wallace. The agnostic, Bob Ingersoll, challenged his brilliant friend, Lew Wallace, to expose Christianity and the Bible as fraud. It has been reported that in the process of investigation, Wallace was converted to Christ and wrote a best-seller book upon which the movie, *Ben Hur,* was made.

Crucifixion of Christ was prophesied in Old Testament

The prophecy of Psalms 22:16 which was written about **a thousand years before Christ** says, "*...they pierced my hands and my feet.*" This is a prophecy of Christ's crucifixion that secular history bears out (even by our calendar dating). Crucifixion was unknown then and was not invented until hundreds of years later. Crucifixion came into its earliest use with the Phoenicians, Greeks, Carthaginians, and Romans. The Emperor Constantine (seeking to establish an enduring empire) did away with it (Constantine was reputed to be the first official pope (pontifex maximus).

The suffering Savior is also prophesied in Isaiah 53:7.

The prophet Daniel wrote of Christ's crucifixion.

"And after threescore and two weeks shall Messiah be cut off..." (Daniel 9:26).

Let truth be heard

You cannot believe in both Creation and evolution at the same time: they have opposite meanings. If one is true, the other is false.

*"...**How long halt ye between two opinions...?** (I Kings 18:21)*

A retired police officer told of his experience of giving polygraph tests (lie detector) for over 30 years. The officer asked each person if they believed in God. Of course, scores of professed atheists said "no" when asked if they believed in the existence of God. The officer said that the polygraph indicated that all of the *professing* atheists had lied (of course, polygraph tests are **not** by a long shot infallible). However, there are some true fools out there (Psalms 14:1).

When this writer was a young man growing up in the textile culture of Greenville, South Carolina, it was not uncommon for some liars to be labeled as "a liar who believes his own lies." The writer thinks that he has met a few like that along the way. It certainly appears that when some liars keep repeating their lies, they began to be convinced that they really are true. For some, perhaps this is a form of believing evolution by proxy. Tell a lie often enough and long enough and others will begin to believe it also!

A wise old proverb says, "To Thine Own Self Be True."

The Bible teaches that the time will come when men will not endure sound doctrine and his itching ears will turn him away from the truth to follow false teachers as well as fables (2 Timothy 4:3-4).

(**Fable:** from nothing - to stellar dust - to green cyanide murky gas - to atoms - to molecules - to amoeba - to monkey – to college professor - to homo sapiens.)

But if any man be ignorant, let him be ignorant (I Corinthians 14:38).

The writer believes that the future eternal existence of both sinners and saints is described in the book of Revelation:

Revelation 22:11: He that is unjust, let him be unjust still: and he which is filthy, let him be filthy still: and he that is righteous, let him be righteous still: and he that is holy, let him be holy still.

If the evolutionists and deniers of Jesus Christ, continue on in their rebellious, arrogant state of unbelief, one day, in a moment of time after they die, they will scream aloud for untold time, "What a fool, What a fool, What a fool, ...too late, too late, too late!"

The writer knows of no worse or a more hopeless end to a person than to have known the claims of the Bible and then having rejected its truth, be sentenced to Hell for all eternity.

Based upon carnal reasoning and shoddy pseudo-science, only a fool would risk the loss of his eternal soul to eternal damnation in Hell fire (Matthew 5:22; 18:8-9; 25:41, 46; Mark 3:29;

118

9:43, 45, 47; 2 Thessalonians 1:9; Jude 6; Revelation 20:14).

Trusting in empty and vain evolution above God's Word is a very cheap price to pay for the loss of a person's soul. The words of Jesus are an ominous warning to the unbeliever.

Mark 8:36, 37: For what shall it profit a man, if he shall gain the whole world, and lose his own soul? Or what shall a man give in exchange for his soul?

An undocumented story worth repeating

"Does evil exist?" The university professor challenged his students with this question. Did God create everything that exists? A student bravely replied, "Yes, he did!"

"God created everything?" the professor asked.

"Yes sir," the student replied.

The professor answered, "If God created everything, then God created evil since evil exists, and according to the principal that our works define who we are, then God is evil." The professor was quite pleased with himself and boasted to the students that he had proven once more that the Christian faith was a myth.

Another student raised his hand and said, "Can I ask you a question professor?"

"Of course," replied the professor.

The student stood up and asked, "Professor, does cold exist?"

The professor replied, "Of course it exists. Have you never been cold?" The students snickered at the young man's question.

The young man replied, "In fact sir, cold does not exist. According to the **laws of physics**, what we consider cold is in reality the absence of heat. Everybody or object is susceptible to study when it has or transmits energy, and heat is what makes a body or matter have or transmit energy. Absolute zero (-460 degrees F) is the total absence of heat. Cold does not exist. We have created this word to describe how we feel if we have not heat."

The student continued. "Professor, does darkness exist?"

The professor responded, "Of course it does."

The student replied, "Once again you are wrong sir. Darkness does not exist either. Darkness is in reality the absence of light. Light we can study, but not darkness. In fact we can use Newton's prism to break white light into many colors and study the various wavelengths of each color. You cannot measure darkness. A simple ray of light can break into a world of darkness and illuminate it. How can you know how dark a certain space is? You measure the amount of light present. Isn't this correct? Darkness is a term used by man to describe what happens when there is no light present."

Finally the young man asked the professor. "Sir, does evil exist?"

Now uncertain, the professor responded, "Of course, as I have already said. We see it every day. It is in the daily example of man's inhumanity to man. It is in the multitude, crime and violence everywhere in the world. These manifestations are nothing else but evil."

To this the student replied, "Evil does not exist sir, or at least it does not exist unto itself. Evil is simply the absence of God. It is just like darkness and cold, a word that man has created to describe the absence of God. God did not created evil. Evil is the result of what happens when man does not have God's love present in his heart. It's like the cold that comes when there is no heat or the darkness that comes when there is no light."

The professor sat down.

The young man's name – Albert Einstein

Atheists are the greatest fools of nature...for they see a world that could not make itself and yet refuse to acknowledge that God made it - (**Matthew Henry**).

Logic of a six-year-old

One day a six-year-old girl was sitting in a classroom. The teacher was going to explain evolution to the children. The teacher asked a little boy, "Tommy, do you see the tree outside?"

"Yes."

"Tommy, do you see the grass outside?"

"Yes."

"Go outside and see if you can see the sky."

"Okay." He returned a few minutes later. "Yes, I saw the sky."

"Did you see God up there?"

"No."

"That's my point. We can't see God because He isn't there. Possibly He just doesn't exist."

A little girl spoke up and wanted to ask Tommy some questions. The teacher agreed and the little girl asked, "Tommy, do you see the tree outside?"

"Yes."

"Tommy, do you see the grass outside?"

"Yes."

"Tommy, do you see the teacher?"

"Yes."

"Do you see her brain?"

"No."

"Then according to what we were taught today in school, she possibly may not even have one!"

Darwin's Repentance: True or False

The writer has read an account of Darwin's last days from several different sources over several decades, but of course, that doesn't necessarily lend veracity to the account. Many writers copy other writers and errors and phony stories are propagated this way. Before you read the following story of Darwin's last days, remember that there are other writers that refute the story as being untrue. Even if untrue, no error can be charged to Scriptures.

The story is told by Lady Hope of Northfield, England, a wonderful Christian woman who often sat at the bedside of Darwin before he died. She herself writes it, and not only is it interesting, it is enlightening. Here is her own words.

"It was one of those glorious autumn afternoons that we sometimes enjoy in England, when I was asked to go and sit with the well-known professor, Charles Darwin. He was almost bedridden for some time before he died. I used to feel when I saw him that his fine presence would have made a grand picture for the Royal Academy; but never did I think so more strongly than on this one particular occasion.

He was sitting up in bed, wearing a soft embroidered, dressing gown of a rich purple shade. Propped up by pillows, he was gazing out on a far-stretching scene of woods and cornfields, which grew in the light of a marvelous sunset. His noble forehead and fine feathers seemed to be lit with pleasure as I entered the room.

He waved his hand toward the window as he pointed toward out the scene beyond, while in the other hand he held an open Bible, he was always studying.

"What are you reading now/" I asked as I was seated by his bedside.

"Hebrews!" he answered—"still Hebrews, The Royal Book, I call it." Then placing his finger on certain passages, he commented on them.

I made some illusion to the strong opinions expressed by many persons on the history of creation, its grandeur and then the treatment of the earliest chapters of the Book of Genesis.

He seemed greatly distressed, and his fingers twitched nervously and a look of anger came over his face as he said, "I was a young man with uninformed ideas. I threw out queries, suggestions, wondering all the time over everything: and to my astonishment the ideas took like wildfire. People made a religion of them."

Then he paused, and after a few more sentences on the holiness of God, and the grandeur of the Book, looking at the Bible which he was holding tenderly all the time. suddenly said, "I have a summer house in the garden which holds about thirty people. It is over there," pointing through the open window, "I want you very much to speak there. I know you read the Bible in villages. Tomorrow afternoon I should like the servants on the place, and a few of the neighbors to gather there. "Will you speak to them?"

"What shall I speak about?" I asked.

"Jesus Christ," he replied, "and His salvation. Is that not the best theme? "And then I want you to sing hymns with them."

The wonderful look of brightness and animation on his face as he said this, I shall never forget, for he added, "If you take the meeting at three o'clock this window will be open, and you will know that I am joining in the singing."

How I wish that I could have made a picture of that fine old man and his beautiful surroundings on that memorable day."

Whether or not the above story is true is of no consequence concerning the truth of God's Word.

The Scriptures are final

JESUS said:

"Search the Scriptures...they testify of me"(John 5:39)

"He (Moses) *wrote of me"(John 5:46)*

"Abraham rejoiced to see my day; and he saw it, and was glad" (John 8:56)

"Before Abraham was, I AM (John 8:58)

John 8:24: I said therefore unto you, that ye shall die in your sins: for if ye believe not that I am he, ye shall die in your sins.

Luke 13:3: I tell you, Nay: but, except ye repent, ye shall all likewise perish.

John 3:3: Jesus answered and said unto him, Verily, verily, I say unto thee, Except a man be born again, he cannot see the kingdom of God.

It is not that the unbeliever "will be" condemned sometimes in the future, but he is "condemned already" (John 3:18, 36). This condition can be likened to a sinner hanging over Hell by a rotten rope awaiting the execution order to be carried out.

The unbeliever needs to flee to God while he still has breath.

The **Apostle Paul** inspired by the Spirit of God said:

Ephesians 2:8, 9: For by grace are ye saved through faith; and that not of yourselves: it is the gift of God: Not of works, lest any man should boast

Romans 10:17: So then faith cometh by hearing, and hearing by the Word of God.

Romans 10:9-11:That if thou shalt confess with thy mouth the Lord Jesus, and shalt believe in thine heart that God hath raised Him from the dead, thou shalt be saved. For with the heart man believeth unto righteousness; and with the mouth confession is made unto salvation. For the Scripture saith, Whosoever believeth on Him shall not be ashamed.

Romans 10:13: For whosoever shall call upon the name of the Lord shall be saved

The French genius **Blaise Pascal** said:

'If you bet there is no God and you win, you win nothing, but if you lose, you lose everything. If you bet there is a God and you win, you win everything, and if you lose, you lose nothing."

Conclusion

Evolutionists claim that evolution is everything; but it is of little use in true science. Keep in mind that evolution of **changes** within kinds is totally different from **origins or beginnings** of kinds. The evolution of origins propagated by evolutionists is best understood as a worldview held by Bible deniers concerning the past but has little application in the present.

John 8:32: And ye shall know the truth, and the truth shall make you free.

The Last Call to Salvation

Forgiveness of sin and salvation can only be found in Jesus Christ (Acts 4:12). There is nowhere else to go (John 6:68). Salvation is free to the believer but it cost God His Dear Son.

Do agnostics, atheists, and evolutionists have something better to offer than Creation and God's free offer of eternal life?

It is an uncontested fact that secular evolution and atheism is a dead-end. There is certainly no future hope or joy associated with the fantasy of evolution. The unbeliever has no peace within his soul. If anyone reading this paper thinks they have something better to offer than God's Salvation (mercy; grace; eternal life), contact the writer. The only offer of evolution and atheism is "fatalism" (no help; no hope; total defeat) that leads to everlasting punishment (Matthew 25:46).

> *Revelation 20:15: And whosoever was not found written in the book of life was cast into the lake of fire.*

Evolutionists and unbelievers are allowing their foolish pride to pave their road to Hell. Deep down within their inner being, they know that they are in great error and in condemnation of God. Their unbelief offers no security from the judgment to come and they have no peace within.

Speaking of unbelievers, the Scriptures say:

> *Romans 3:3: for what if some did not believe? Shall their unbelief make the faith of God without effect?*

While there is life, there is hope for the evolutionists.

God gave the record of His Son and anyone disbelieving that record (The Bible) is calling God a liar (I John 5:10). For unbelief in God's Word, there is never any pardon.

Dennis Helton
200 Home Place Drive
Easley, SC 29640

Bibliography

American Dictionary of the English Language-- Noah Webster 1828, Foundation For American Christian Education, PO Box 27035, San Francisco, California 94127

Authorized King James Bible of 1611.

*Big Daddy,*Chick Publications, P.O. Box 662, Chino, CA 91708-0662 USA

Biblical Evangelist, 5717 Pine Drive, Raleigh, NC 27606-8947

Blackstone, W.E. *Jesus Is Coming,* Fleming H. Revell Company, Old Tappan, NewJersey

Carroll, J.M.,*The Trail of Blood,* Ashland Avenue Baptist Church, 163 N. Ashland Ave., Lexington, KY 40502, Copyright 1931.

Cloud, David W., *Way of Life Encyclopedia of the Bible & Christianity,* Way of Life Literature, 1219 North Harns Road, Oak Harbor, Washington 98277, copyright 1993.

*Days of Praise,*Institute for Creation Research, Santee, California 92071

Eddleman, H. Leo, *Last Things.*

Foxe, John, *Foxe's Book of Martyrs,* Whitaker House, Pittsburg and Colfax Streets, Springdale, Pennsylvania 15144.

Gipp, Samuel C. *An Understandable History of the Bible,* Copyright 1987 Samuel C. Gipp, Bible Believers Bookstore, 1252 Aurora Road, Macedonia, Ohio 44056

Greene, Oliver B.*Bible Prophecy*, The Gospel Hour, Inc., Box 2024, Greenville, SC 29602

Halff, Dr. Charles ,*Message of the Christian Jew,* May-June 1998

"Some Prophecies That Never Came True", Dave Hunt.

Hardison, D. M., *Circuit Rider News,* Jan-March, 2010

Hefley, James and Marti, *Where in the World are the Jews Today?*

Hislop, Alexander, *The Two Babylons,* Loizeaux Brothers, Neptune, New Jersey.

Hunt, Dave, *A Woman Rides the Beast*, Harvest House Publishers, Eugene, Oregon 97402.

Hunt, Dave, *Peace Prosperity and the Coming Holocaust,* Harvest House Publishers, Eugene, Oregon 97402.

Huse, Scott M*The Collapse of Evolution*, Baker Books, Grand Rapids, Michigan 49516

Institute for Creation Research, P.O. Box 2667, El Cajon, CA 92021-0667

Ironside, H.A. *Holiness, The False and the True,* Loizeaux Brothers, Neptune, N.J..

Jones, Bob Sr., *False Religions,* Bob Jones University Press, Greenville, S.C..

Larkin, Clarence, *Dispensational Truth,* Rev. Clarence Larkin Est., 2802 N. Park Ave., Philadelphia 32, Pa, Copyrighted 1918.

Larkin, Clarence,*The Spirit World*, Erwin W. Moyer Co., Printer, Philadelphia, PA.

McBeth, Leon, *Strange New Religions*, Broadman Press, Nashville, TN, Copyright 1977.

McDowell & Stewart, *Handbook of Today's Religions*, Thomas Nelson Publishers, 1983.

McElveen, Floyd, *Christianity: Sense or Nonsense.*

Pictorial Bible Dictionary,Zondervan Publishing House, Grand Rapids, Michigan

Riplinger, Gail A., *New Age Bible Versions*, A.V. Publications Corp., P.O. Box 280, Ararat, VA 24053, Copyright by G.A. Riplinger, 1993.

Seiss, J. A., *The Gospel in the Stars,* Kregel Publications, P.O. Box 2607 , Grand Rapids, MI 49501.

Smith, Wilbur *Smith's Bible Dictionary*, Barbour and Company, Inc., 164 Mill Street, Westwood, New Jersey 07675

Strong, James, *Strong's Exhaustive Concordance of the Bible.*

Sword of the Lord, April 17, 1998, "News and Views", Hugh Pyle.

Times Examiner, The 44 Pine Knoll Dr., Suite E-2, Greenville, SC 29609

Vine, W.E., *Expository Dictionary of New Testament Words*, Fleming H. Revell Co., Westwood, N.J..

Webster's Ninth New Collegiate Dictionary.

Walvoord, John F. *Major Bible Prophecies,* Zondervan Publishing House, Grand Rapids, Michigan 49530, Copyright 1991 by John F. Walvoord

Wilson & Weldon, *Occult Shock and Psychic Forces*, Master Books, San Diego, Calif.

Woychuk, N. A., *The Indestructible Nation*, Scripture Memory Fellowship International, P.O. Box 24551, St. Louis, Missouri 63141.

ABOUT THE AUTHOR

The writer was born in Greenville, SC in 1934 and was a lifetime resident with the exception of two years in the US Army (Fort Jackson, S.C. and Fort Carson, Colorado) and two years residence in Florida.

After separation (honorably) from the US Army, the writer returned to Greenville, SC and married at age 27 to Christine Moore, an old acquaintance from an adjacent neighborhood. The Lord blessed us with six daughters, Debbie, Donna, Dale, Denise, Deree, and Dena.

A short time after marriage, the writer was convicted of his lost condition as a sinner and after a miserable time under conviction the writer confessed his sin and lost condition to God and was saved.

The writer was 40 years of age when he began attending college (3 years, no diploma).

The writer retired as a chemical technologist from Morton International Chemical Company in 1996. Before retirement, the writer had the urge to write on Bible subjects and wished that he had more time to study. Upon retirement, the writer bought a computer and became a novice writer.

The writer now resides in Easley, S.C.

D. Helton has written several documents and books, as well as the book, "Jesus is God," available here:
http://www.theoldpathspublications.com/Pages/Auth ors/Helton.htm#God